Keeping the Knot Tied

Keeping the Knot Tied

The Covenant of Marriage

Larry A. Bell, M.S.; L.P.C.

XULON PRESS

Xulon Press
2301 Lucien Way #415
Maitland, FL 32751
407.339.4217
www.xulonpress.com

Paperback ISBN-13: 978-1-66284-172-9
Ebook ISBN-13: 978-1-66284-173-6

DEDICATION

On December 30, 1972, my wife, Deanna, and I entered the Covenant of Marriage.

We have now been committed to each other for forty-eight years. Deanna is a gift from God to me. Her love, support and encouragement have kept me on track through many trials and tribulations. We are a good team. I am thankful to have such a loving and faithful wife.

God has blessed our marriage with two terrific children. Jessica, my favorite daughter and Kenan, my favorite son. Kenan is married to Bethany, my favorite daughter-in-law.

We now enjoy the exceptional blessings of five grandchildren: Violet, Sophia, Ivory Jane, Hudson and Westray.

This book is dedicated with gratitude to my bride, Deanna. I cannot imagine what my life would be like without her. She is a Godly woman, an amazing Mom and an incredible Grandmother. I love her with all my heart!!!

*"He who finds a good wife
finds a good thing and obtains
favor from the LORD."
[Proverbs 18:22 – ESV]*

I have definitely found a good wife and have obtained favor from YHWH!!!

TABLE OF CONTENTS

PRIMARY ACKNOWLEDGEMENT

I was born on December 1, 1950, and I was 'born again' in August of 1976. God convinced me that I was separated from Him, and He graciously extended the gift of salvation to me based upon what His Son, YESHUA, had accomplished at the cross. I called on His Name and asked Him to forgive me of my sin, come into my life and make me a new person. That decision changed the entire direction of my life. I am eternally grateful for His grace and mercy. My prayer is that this book will bring honor to YHWH and portray an accurate representation of His inspired Word.

SPECIAL THANKS

S teve Felder is an amazingly gifted Pastor and Teacher. I had the privilege of ministering with him during the foundational years of Fellowship Bible Church in Bridgeport, West Virginia. He and I initially worked together on the basics for this Model of Marriage. The model became an integral part of my counseling with hundreds of couples over the last four decades. A special thanks to Steve for all God taught me through his ministry.

INTRODUCTION

In June 2011 I lead a group of twenty-five people to explore and study in Israel.

Accompanying me on this journey were my wife, Deanna, my son, Kenan, his girlfriend, Bethany, and my nine-year old granddaughter, Violet. Kenan and I stayed together and the three ladies shared a room. As I was preparing for the trip, my son asked my advice because his desire was to propose to Bethany in Israel. I was so excited for him!!! When I lead trips to Israel, we share devotionals at each of the major locations. My suggestion was for Kenan to present the devotional in Cana of Galilee. I indicated he could read the passage in John 2 and then expound upon the text. This chapter records where YESHUA Himself honored the Covenant of Marriage by participating in a marriage celebration in Cana. HE accentuated His blessing on this marriage by conducting HIS first miracle of changing the water to wine. This would be the first in a series of miracles designed to prove that YEHSHUA is the Messiah. After Kenan explained this particular section of scripture, I suggested that he conclude his devotional with the comments that the Apostle Paul wrote in Ephesians 5:32 —which characterize marriage as being a 'mystery'. He could explain that the 'mystery' alluded to by Paul connected the Covenant of Marriage and the ministry of Christ. Christ is the Bridegroom and the

Church is His Bride. Now the only remaining mystery is: "Bethany will you marry me?" He liked my idea and decided to proceed with the plan.

When we arrived in Israel our first night was spent on the Sea of Galilee. The Sea of Galilee is actually a lake that is thirteen miles long by eight miles wide. It is the lowest freshwater lake in the world at 650" below sea level and the scenery is spectacular!!

Our LORD spent two-thirds of His public ministry in and around this lake.

Peter, Andrew, James, and John fished on this lake. YESHUA calmed a storm on this lake and walked upon the water here.

I always have sleep difficulties the first night of international travel and was awakened around 2:00 a.m. due to jet lag. Kenan was also up early due to understandable nervousness and anticipation. He decided to put the finishing touches on the devotional that he would present toward the end of our first day of touring. We both concluded our studies with a spectacular view of sunrise over the Sea of Galilee. Biblical history comes alive in Galilee!!

Later that afternoon, after he concluded the devotional at Cana, he literally got down on one knee in front of Bethany and said "The only remaining mystery is, Bethany will you marry me?" Thankfully she said "Yes"! June 7, 2011, is certainly a day that is forever etched in my memory.

Nearly one year later, on May 5, 2012, I was gifted with the pleasure of officiating the wedding. It was the best speaking opportunity that I've ever experienced in my life. Being invited to be part of the ceremony which culminated in Kenan Nathaniel Bell and Bethany Jane Casper entering the Covenant of Marriage was truly a blessing beyond compare.

In this book I intend to explore the Covenant of Marriage from a Biblical standpoint. I am a Licensed Professional Counselor in the States of West Virginia and Virginia. I have worked with hundreds of couples in marital counseling. I have discovered that many problems develop over a period of time because people forget to pay attention to the basic principles that God has laid out for us in His Word. I honestly believe that if couples will follow the principles put forth in the Bible, that their marriage will be strengthened. The scriptures are therapeutic and can bring about healing and reconciliation that is needed by so many.

On that day I challenged Kenan and Bethany to establish an unwavering Commitment to each other. I also accentuated that it was essential to invest a great deal of energy in maturing their level of Intimacy. If they remain steadfast in these first two components of a vibrant marriage they then will enjoy Passion in the way our Creator intended – which is the unique celebration of the Covenant of Marriage. Marriage is a Covenant Commitment.

MODEL OF MARRIAGE

The triangle is the strongest multi-sided figure known to man. I utilize the triangle in various teachings. The Model of Marriage that I use in counseling is based on a triangle. The diagram that follows will demonstrate the basic components of marriage that are crucial for a stable and vibrant marriage.

Moses penned these words approximately 3500 years ago:

"Therefore, shall a man LEAVE his father
and his mother, and CLEAVE unto his wife:
and they shall be ONE FLESH."
[Genesis 2:24 [KJV]

In this section of the Original Testament Moses indicated three terms associated with the Covenant of Marriage: 'Leave', 'Cleave', and 'One Flesh'. The triangle diagram shows 'Leave' at the base of the triangle, 'Cleave' on the left side, and 'One Flesh' on the right side.

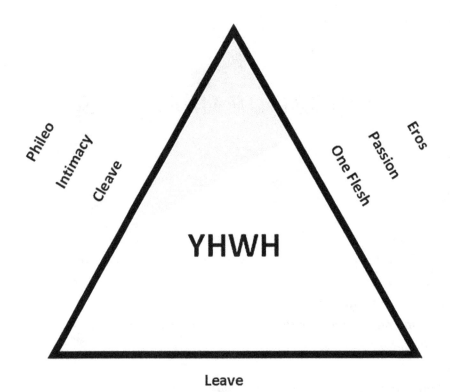

Leave

Commitment

Agape

These three basic concepts will be further explained below:

> ➢ *'Leave' - 'Commitment' - 'Agape'*
> ➢ *'Cleave' - 'Intimacy' - 'Phileo'*
> ➢ *'One Flesh' - 'Passion' - 'Eros'*

I will explore each of these components and how they are expressed within the Covenant of Marriage. Each side of the triangle must be intact and functioning for the marriage to remain strong. If there are any cracks on any side of the triangle the marriage relationship will suffer to some degree. In the center of the triangle is YHWH. YHWH is the covenant name of God that He gave to Moses in Exodus 3:14. Our GOD is the One Who created and designed us as humans. HE is the One Who originated the Covenant of Marriage. If we keep GOD at the center of our marriage, we are inviting His Divine Presence to intercede on behalf of our marriage. HE will teach and guide us regarding the fulfillment of our covenant obligations by the indwelling of the Holy Spirit.

The society of the United States of America is in the process of losing its moral compass. The USA was founded upon Biblical principles. We are witnessing a social contagion in our country that is bent towards immorality and the denial of absolute truth. It is apparent that our society is experiencing a plague of Moral Confusion, Sexual Confusion, and Gender Confusion. GOD is not the author of confusion. The USA is in the midst of a spiritual battle. This is proving to have a devastating impact on the covenant of marriage. The Biblical foundation of a traditional marriage is being undermined. If this continues, our society will collapse. We need a return to basics. A realization that adherence to Biblical principles is a requirement to receive the blessings of YHWH.

Israel experienced similar circumstances in the 6th century B.C. Because they ignored Biblical principles, they invited the judgment of YHWH. YHWH spoke to His people through the prophet Jeremiah. These words demonstrate the necessity of reassessing our current condition and acknowledgment that we can be restored as a nation if we return to our foundational principles based on the truth of the scriptures. I am praying we return to the very basics of faith.

"Thus says the LORD;
Stand by the roads, and
look, and ask for the ancient
paths, where the good way is;
and walk in it, and find rest for
your souls. But they said,

"We will not walk in it."
[Jeremiah 6:16 – ESV]

ASSESSMENT OF THE STATE OF MARRIAGE IN THE UNITED STATES

[A Comparison to Ancient Rome]

These three primary components of marriage will be explained and discussed in the framework of a Covenant Commitment. In the United States we are witnessing a major deterioration of the traditional family unit. Divorce rates are extremely high. One of the primary reasons for the high divorce rate is that couples have exchanged the concept of covenant for a contract mentality, like a business type of arrangement. If a spouse fails to complete the 'contract', the marriage is readily expendable and dissolved. Some studies indicate that the United States is approaching a 50% rate of divorce. The ancient Roman Empire was one of the most powerful empires to ever exist. The Romans exerted their influence on the world from 27 B.C. through 476 A.D. One of the primary reasons for the demise of the Roman Empire was the degeneration of the traditional family unit. British Historian Edward Gibbon [1737-1794] wrote his book entitled "History of the Decline and Fall of the Roman Empire". Gibbon offered five primary reasons for the demise of the Roman Empire.

- *First: The rapid increase of divorce, with the undermining of the sanctity of the home, which is the basis of society.*

- *Second: Higher and higher taxes, and the spending of public money on bread and circuses.*

- *Third: The mad craze for pleasure and sports becoming more exciting and more brutal every year.*

- *Fourth: The building of gigantic armies to fight external enemies, when the most deadly enemy, the decadence of the people, lay within.*

- *Fifth: The decay of religion; faith fading into mere form, losing touch with life, and becoming impotent to guide it.*

- *Article by Andrew Webb on biblebased.wordpress.com / google [2014]*

Mr. Gibbon listed the demise of the traditional family unit and the accelerated prevalence of divorce as the leading cause for the decline of the Roman Republic. There are many political currents attempting to re-engineer the traditional family unit in the USA. The unscientific notion that there are now more than 70 different gender identifiers is troubling.

Naturally, this affects the composition of the family unit. The National Human Genome Research Institute indicates that all humans are 99.9% identical. The small differential attributes to sex, height, skin tone, eye color, type of hair, etc. 99.07 % of humanity has an "XX" or an "XY" chromosome. The remaining .03% have a genetic anomaly or medical malfunction.

The design and intent of our Creator is the binary sexual system. Simply stated:

"So, God created man in His own image, In the image of God He created him: male and female He created them".
[Genesis 1:27 – ESV]

"But from the beginning of creation, God made them male and female."
[Mark 10:6 – ESV]

The biblical design for marriage and family is for one male and one female to enter into the Covenant of Marriage. It is in that traditional framework that children have the best chances of thriving. In our country people have the legal right to same sex marriage and a variety of family configurations. That does not negate the intent of our Creator from a Biblical perspective. Legal rights certainly do not automatically equate to the moral standards expounded in the Bible. Activists have been very successful in reframing their argument.

They removed their arguments from a moral framework and reframed their argument in the context of civil rights.

The other four reasons highlighted by Gibbon are applicable to America today in my opinion. The second cause for the demise of Rome proposed by Gibbon was the fact that the Roman government required increasingly higher levels of taxation from the citizens. A large amount of this tax money was spent on 'panem et circenses' which translates into 'bread and circuses. Bread was provided in abundance and at no charge in Rome. That may sound positive on the surface, but it decreased the need to work. Fewer people working meant more taxes were required from those who did work. That had a direct impact on Roman marriages and families.

I have had the opportunity to travel throughout many parts of the ancient Roman empire. It is incredible to observe the theaters, amphitheaters, coliseums, and hippodromes that are prominently preserved throughout the empire. Romans could enjoy sporting events like chariot races or gladiator fights at no charge. The amount of money needed to provide free bread and public entertainment became exorbitant. The Roman leadership believed that if you were able to meet the needs of the general population in these two specific areas you could control the population. The poorer people would be content with having their basic food requirements met. Rome would keep the populace busy with entertainment. Provision of bread and circus reduced the possibility of revolt against the Roman leadership.

Is America on this same course followed by Rome? Nearly 60,000,000 people in America receives some type of welfare support. The population of America is 328,000,000.

Nearly 20% of the population is on welfare support. The USA is certainly wealthy enough to pay for the needs of those who truly are unable to help themselves. There are a significant number of people who could work, but choose not to work and that creates increased taxation from those who do work. This is a major source of stress on marriages and the family. The tax rates are increasing on the typical American wage earner. Financial difficulty is a major cause of marital discord and frankly our politicians are contributing to the problem. The fact that the federal government takes too much of our paychecks to support an ever-growing welfare system contributes to high levels of stress in marriages. We are witnessing too much 'dough' being spent on too much 'bread'. And couples often compound the problem by personal financial mismanagement. There is only a certain amount of money available to be taxed. With the increasing popularity of socialism and an entitlement mentality, we can expect family financial stress to continue to burgeon. This will quite likely increase the divorce rate in the United States.

*The problem with socialism
is that you eventually run
out of other people's money.
[British Prime Minister –
Margaret Thatcher]*

In the USA we have also seen the government subsidization of entertainment which costs billions of tax dollars. Do people in our country have a constitutional right to own an smartphone? I can't find that anywhere in the constitution. You might argue that the cell phone is not entertainment, but I would disagree. How much time is spent on cell phones with entertaining activities? Surfing the internet, music, pornography, and mind-numbing games are definitely entertainment activities for some people. Local, state and federal governments subsidize the National Basketball Association, the National Football League and Major League Baseball. If people have televisions and cell phones, they can basically be kept entertained. Seems very similar to what history has taught us from ancient Rome. When the government provides food and entertainment then people can choose to become lackadaisical about working. Over time this creates an entitlement mentality that is detrimental to society and marriages. There seems to be a common connection between the deterioration of Rome and what is transpiring in America – 'bread and circuses'.

The federal government has an insatiable appetite for taxation which results in unnecessary and wasteful spending. High levels of taxation extract disposable income from families and create budgetary stress for families. For decades our politicians have demonstrated reckless spending patterns that have robbed resources from American families.

If we, as individuals, managed our checking accounts like the federal government squanders our tax dollars – we would be in jail! Financial *stress is one of the top five factors which results in the need for couples to pursue marital counseling. I have personally worked with couples who accumulated $60,000.00 of credit card debt very early in their marriage. They were lured into only paying the minimum payment per month. If they continued that pattern, they would likely never pay that debt off. Newlyweds often invite financial stress by thinking they must immediately have a full house of furniture, the best cars and trinkets. They fail to realize that their parents have worked decades to have a house full of good furniture.*

Impulsive spending and misuse of credit creates enormous pressure on couples. Patience is a path of wisdom to pursue. Adhering to a budget is essential and therapeutic.

"Government's view of the economy could be summed up in a few short phrases: If it moves, tax it. If it keeps moving, regulate it. If it stops moving, subsidize it.". [The 39th President of the United States – Ronald Reagan]

According to the United States Government Accounting Office the USA currently has a national debt of nearly $27,000,000,000,000. If we operated our personal accounts like the politicians are managing our tax money we would go to jail. The politicians in the House and Senate have been spending money they do not have for decades. Congressman and Senators are simply writing bad checks. This causes terrific financial stress on many marriages. The government takes too much money from our

paychecks and financial stress significantly contributes to marital diffi-
culties. It was true in Rome 2,000 years ago and is applicable today.

Financial stressors can become so overwhelming that couples are choosing
to opt out of their marriage commitment.

The third reason that Gibbon addressed in the decline of the Roman
Republic was the 'mad craze for pleasure, sports becoming every year
more exciting and more brutal'. America is becoming an increasingly
hedonistic society. The quest for pleasure and sensuality dominates tele-
vision programming, the movie industry, the music industry and is
pervasive on the internet. When I was in college in the late sixties and
early seventies the philosophy of: "If it feels good – do it!!" was ubiqui-
tous. Many people continued to live that type of lifestyle for decades. This
attitude is unhealthy for being committed to marriage. Sexual immo-
rality reached epidemic proportions. My first sociology professor in the
spring of 1969 stated: "In the next ten years, sex would be as common
as a handshake". That prediction basically became a reality. With that
type of sexual permissiveness, the United States experienced a rise in
sexually transmitted diseases. Unplanned pregnancies skyrocketed and
the abortion industry gained a foothold in American society. Adultery
levels increased and subsequently the divorce rate began to climb. People
became less willing to commit to marriage and the number of couples
living together without entering the Covenant of Marriage became more
in vogue in the eyes of many.

A 2019 study conducted by the Pew Research Center discovered that 69%
of people surveyed have a positive view of cohabitation even if the couple
never marries. 16% believed that cohabitation was acceptable only if the
couple planned to marry. Only 14% believed that cohabitation without
being in the Covenant of Marriage was never acceptable. This huge shift
in perspective over the last five decades has had a tremendously adverse
effect on the Covenant of Marriage.

Has there ever been a more self-centered generation than we currently are witnessing in the USA? This generation is the most self-photographed in the history of the world.

Teenagers have developed an habitual obsession with 'selfies'. Being self-absorbed is contraindicated in a marriage. The idea of being the center of attention leads to selfish lifestyles. We must focus on meeting the needs of our spouse in the Covenant of Marriage. A marriage functions more positively if both the husband and the wife place the other person in a position of priority. Marriage is a divinely originated partnership. A prideful and self-centered attitude will dilute the strength of the individual commitment to the marriage alliance.

Want a bad marriage"
Put yourself first.
Want a good marriage?
Put your spouse first.
Want a great marriage?
Put God first.
[Soldier of Christ
Ronnie Chrisman]

Gibbon addressed the effect of the excessive expenditures of the Roman government on their military as fourth consideration for the demise of Rome. This reason is an extension of government spending that detracts from individual household income. Obviously, we need a strong military to protect our country. Any fat that could be trimmed from the budgets of perpetual social programs could be beneficial to married couples in somewhat reducing the financial stressors that cause turmoil. Gibbon indicated that Rome became primarily focused upon external enemies and failed to pay heed to the moral decay within the Roman society.

I believe that there are definite parallels that are applicable to the United States currently.

Moral decay persists at alarming levels. The last verse in the Book of Judges aptly describes what I observe to be transpiring in our country.

> *"Everyone did what was right*
> *in his own eyes."*
> *[Judges 21:25 – ESV]*

What became apparent in Israel 3,000 years ago during the time period when Judges reigned, is becoming the prevailing mentality in the United States. People do not want to accept 'absolute truth' and our society is trending rapidly towards relativism.

Gallop polling, which was completed in May 2018, indicated an alarming trend in the reduction of moral values in America. 49% of those responding to the survey rated the state of morals in the U.S. as being 'poor'. 37% of those responding rated the state of morals in the U.S. as 'only fair' and a paltry 14% rated the morality in the U.S. as being 'excellent' or 'good'. Contributing factors discussed in this survey included the rise of 'self-indulgent, hedonistic behaviors and lifestyles'. [Andy Burges @ delmarvano. com – 01/31/2019] This level of moral decay permeates our society and has devastating consequences to the Covenant of Marriage and families.

Never laugh at your
wife's choices…
You were one of them!!!

In 1796 President George Washington wrote these words in his farewell address to the country that he was instrumental in forming:

"Of all the dispositions and habits which lead to political prosperity, religion and morality are indispensable supports. And let us with caution indulge the supposition that morality can be maintained without religion. Whatever may be conceded to the influence of refined education on minds of peculiar structure, reason and experience both forbid us to expect that national morality can prevail in the exclusion of religious principle." [Andy Burges @ delmarvanow.com]

*"Blessed is the nation whose God
is the LORD…"
[Psalm 33:12 – ESV]*

YHWH, the God of the Bible, is being rejected by a significant number of people.

Our political structure is infected with corruption on both sides of the aisle. Hatred, wickedness and violence have been nurtured and even encouraged. It reminds me of the days of Noah when wickedness and violence increased so much that YHWH judged the entire world. These words written 3500 years ago should resound in the U.S. today:

*"The LORD saw that the wickedness of man
was great in the earth, and that every intention
of the thoughts of his heart was only evil continually."
[Genesis 6:5]*

*"Now the earth was corrupt in God's sight,
and the earth was filled with violence. And God
saw the earth, and behold, it was corrupt, for
all flesh had corrupted their way on the earth."
[Genesis 6:11]*

If this country that I love continues to reject YHWH and diminishes or eliminates freedom of religious expression for Christians, we are headed for destruction just like ancient Rome. I know some people scoff at the notion that we may lose our Freedom of Religion but it is quite apparent that followers of YESHUA are under attack.

The fifth and final point that Gibbon made that directly impacted the decline of the Roman Empire: "The decay of religion: faith fading into mere form, losing touch with life and becoming impotent to guide it." This is of primary importance when considering the declining lack of commitment to the Covenant of Marriage in our culture. We derive the entire concept of marriage from the scriptures and those scriptures have been directly inspired by YHWH Himself. The Founding Fathers of our country utilized Biblical principles in the formation of America. It has been said that America is in a 'post-Christian' state. I believe that to be true. America is wavering in its commitment to YHWH and His principles. We have entered a phase in American history where people profess diversity and inclusiveness. These people who worship at the altar of 'political correctness' are on the front lines of attacking those who are disciples of YESHUA. Biblical morality is called into question and labeled as 'bigotry'. The Christian church is under attack and according to the scriptures this will continue to worsen as we enter the 'last days'. We see a decline in the belief of the existence of God. We have a society that does not want to accept the premise of absolute truth. This type of mentality is having a disastrous impact on the traditional marriage and family unit.

God created male and female and instituted the Covenant of Marriage for their well-being.

When God is denied, and HIS word is ignored, we can only expect the deterioration of marriages and families.

It is imperative that we learn from history and not succumb as victims to the mistakes of the past. We must return to honoring the very basics of the truth of the word of God as it applies to the Covenant of Marriage. Moses wrote these words 3500 years ago:

> *"Therefore, shall a man leave his father and mother, and shall cleave unto his wife; and they shall be flesh." [Genesis 2:24 KJV]*

➢ *'Leave' will correlate to Commitment and Agape*

➢ *'Cleave' will correspond to Intimacy and Phileo*

➢ *'One Flesh' will connote with Passion and Eros*

A return to the foundational basics of the Covenant of Marriage that were instituted by YHWH with Adam and Eve is essential. A commitment to the Covenant of Marriage is imperative for our culture to survive and thrive. We need to return to the basics and follow the original design of our Creator.

LEAVE – COMMITMENT – AGAPE

The first covenant to be instituted by YHWH concerning human relationships is the Covenant of Marriage. YESHUA Himself emphasized the importance of the covenant of marriage in the Gospel of Matthew:

> "And He answered and said to them,
> "Have you not read that He Who
> made them male and female, and said,
> 'For this reason, a man shall leave
> his mother and father and be joined
> to his wife and the two shall become
> one flesh. So then, they are no longer
> two but one flesh. Therefore, what God
> has joined together, let not man separate."
> [Matthew 19:4-6]

The word covenant in the Hebrew literally means 'to cut'. One of the most illustrative passages dealing with the description of a covenant relationship is recorded in Genesis 15.

> "And he [Abram] said, "LORD God, how shall I know that I will
> inherit it? [referring to the Land of Promise] So He said to him,

'Bring Me a three-year-old heifer, a three-year-old ram, a turtle-dove, and a young pigeon.' Then he brought all these to Him and cut them in two, down the middle, and placed each piece opposite the other; but he did not cut the birds in two. And when the vultures came down on the carcasses, Abram drove them away. Now when the sun was going down, a deep sleep fell upon Abram; and behold, horror and great darkness fell upon him. Then He said to Abram: "Know certainly that your descendants will be strangers in a land that is not theirs and will serve them, and they will afflict them four hundred years. And also, the nation whom they serve I will judge; afterward they shall come out with great possessions. Now as for you, you shall go to your fathers in peace; you shall be buried at a good old age. But in the fourth generation they shall return here, for the iniquity of the Amorites is not yet complete." And it came to pass, when the sun went down and it was dark, that behold, there appeared a smoking oven and a burning torch that passed between those pieces. On that same day the LORD made a covenant with Abram saying; "to your descendants I have given this land, from the river of Egypt to the great river, the river Euphrates – the Kenites, the Kenezzites, the Kadmonites, the Hittites, the Perizzites, the Rephaim, the Amorites, the Canaanites, the Girgashites, and the Jebusites." [Genesis 15:8-16 – ESV]

In many cultures around the world including Celtic, Hindu & Egyptian weddings – the hands of the bride and groom are literally tied together. This demonstrates the couple's commitment to each other and their new bond as a married couple.
This is the origination of the phrase:

"Tying the knot".
[Credit: "the knot" website]

A covenant is to be entered into with the idea of fulfillment. YHWH promised Abram that his descendants would eventually inherit the Land of Promise. We see that promise was fulfilled six centuries later when Moses lead Israel out of the bondage of Egypt. In 1400 B.C.

General Joshua invaded the Land of Promise, and the tribes of Israel resettled the land.

Israel experienced eviction from the land due to disobedience 605-586 BCE as they were exiled to Babylon. The Israelites returned from exile seventy years later. Once again in 70 AD Israel experienced exile under the Romans. We witnessed an incredible fulfillment of the covenant between YHWH and Abram in 1917. The Balfour Declaration enabled Jews to once again have their residence in the Land of Promise. YHWH had entered a covenant with Abram. Abram had HIS word that the details of the covenant would transpire. This covenant has withstood the test of time as YHWH is always true to HIS word.

In this day and age, we do not cut animals into halves and offer them as sacrifices.

This Biblical illustration of YHWH entering the covenant with Abram serves as a reminder that when we do enter a covenant, and invite the LORD to be present, the vows should be exchanged reverently and solemnly.

Entering into a covenant requires an exchange of vows. Moses accentuated the wholehearted nature of a vow in the last book of the Pentateuch – Deuteronomy:

"If you make a vow to the LORD
your God, you shall not delay
fulfilling it, for the LORD your
God will surely require it of you,
and you will be guilty of sin. But
if you refrain from vowing, you will
not be guilty of sin. You shall be
careful to do what has passed your lips,
for you have voluntarily vowed to the
LORD your God what you have
promised with your mouth."
[Deuteronomy 23:21-23 – ESV]

When we enter the Covenant of Marriage, in the presence of YHWH and other witnesses, we should do so with the expectation of completing the vows. We honor YHWH by honoring the covenant. It appears that many people today are not viewing the Covenant of Marriage as a spiritual covenant with their Creator. Instead, they are extraordinarily flippant about the covenant and treat it merely like a business deal. If the business deal sours, in their perspective, they have no apparent problem in dissolving what they perceive as a failed 'contract'.

The following are several examples of couples who demonstrated a considerably lackadaisical attitude towards the Covenant of Marriage. Country western singer Kenny Chesney met Renee Zellweger in January 2005. They were married in May 2005. He wrote the song: "You Had Me at Hello" which was supposedly inspired by Zellweger. Sadly, after four months the couple dissolved their marriage by annulment. They clearly did not have the concept of covenant from a spiritual standpoint in mind from the exchange of vows.

Annulment is a perplexing term for me to comprehend. "An annulment is a legal procedure that cancels a marriage. An annulled marriage is erased from a legal perspective, and it declares that the marriage never technically existed and was never valid" {Merriam-Webster Dictionary}. So, the couple enters the Covenant of Marriage, and through some legal jargon the Covenant never occurred.

The Top 20 Most Expensive Engagement Rings

#1 – Mariah Carey - $10,000,000
#2 - Blue Diamond by Bvlgari - $9,500,000
#3 - Elizabeth Taylor - $8,800,000
#4 - Kim Kardashian - $8,000,0000
#5 - Anna Kournikova - $5,400,000
#6 – Beyonce - $5,000,000
#7 - Paris Hilton - $4,700,000
#8 - Grace Kelly - $4,600,000
#9 - Jennifer Lopez - $4,500,000
#10 – Melania Trump - $3,000,000
#11 - Jacqueline Kennedy Onassis - $2,600,000
#12 – Blake Lively - $2,500,000
#13 – Kate Upton - $1,500,000
#14 – Jennifer Aniston - $1,000,000
#15 – Angeline Jolie - $1,000,000
#16 – Gabrielle Union - $1,000,000
#17 – Iggy Azalea - $500,000
#18 – Lady Gaga - $500,000
#19 – Kate Middleton - $500,000
#20 – Cardi B - $500,000
[WealthyGorilla.com]

Another listless example towards the Covenant of Marriage is exemplified by Kim Kardashian and Kris Humphries whose marriage lasted 72

days. Michelle Phillips and Dennis Hopper were married a total of six days. Nicolas Cage and Erika Koike barely completed their honeymoon and terminated their marriage on the fourth day.

Brittney Spears and Jason Alexander were married in 2004 and their marriage 'endured' a total of 56 hours.

Dennis Rodman may have exhibited the most blatant mockery of the marriage covenant in 1996. He declared himself to be bisexual. He purchased a custom-made wedding dress and married himself! Unfortunately, we find this lack of seriousness and irreverence replicated throughout our society.

When we enter the Covenant of Marriage it should be with an absolute determination that we intend to fulfill the vows we exchange. In I Corinthians 13:7 Paul states that love 'always perseveres' [NIV]. That terminology suggests a level of steadfastness. There is an enduring expectation that comes along with exchanging vows in the context of the Covenant of Marriage. It is like deciding to go on a trip.

You make plans and set the itinerary. You begin your trip with the goal in mind of reaching your destination. On the road you may experience car difficulties, roadwork delays, potholes, and drivers who are texting. But you stay the course. You exit the highway to refuel or refresh but you do not turn around. When we exchange vows and say, "I do", we then began a fantastic covenant journey that is designed by YHWH to endure the test of time.

Did you know that 17 tons of gold are made into wedding rings each year in the USA? [Credit: 'the knot' website]

The Guinness Book of Records indicates that the longest verifiable marriage on record was between Herbert Fisher and Zelmyra Fisher. They were married in North Carolina on May 13, 1924. Their marriage endured until February 27, 2011, when Mr. Fisher passed away. Their marriage lasted an incredible 86 years and 290 days. The Fisher marriage proved to be steadfast and they fulfilled the portion of their vows that stated, "Til death do us part".

The ultimate depiction of the covenant nature of the marriage vows is presented by Paul in Ephesians:

> *"Husbands, love your wives, as Christ loved the church and Gave Himself up for her, that HE might sanctify her, having cleansed her by the washing of water with the word, so that He might present the church to Himself in splendor, without spot or wrinkle or any such thing, that she might be holy and without blemish. In the same way husbands should love their wives as their own bodies. He who loves his wife loves himself. For no one ever hated his own flesh but nourishes and cherishes it, just as Christ does the church, because we are members of HIS body. Therefore, a man shall leave his father and mother and hold fast to his wife, and the two shall become one flesh. This mystery is profound, and I am saying it refers to Christ and the church." [Ephesians 5:25-32 - ESV]*

In this analogy Christ is the Bridegroom and the church is His Bride.

Christ entered the New Covenant by shedding HIS blood. As previously mentioned, the Hebrew word for covenant literally means 'to cut'. Christ was 'cut' four specific ways in order to seal this covenant. HE was beaten and 'cut' by a Roman whip, HIS head was 'cut' by a crown crafted from thorns and pressed upon HIS brow, HIS hands and feet were pierced and 'cut' by iron spikes, and finally HIS side was pierced and 'cut' by the sword of a Roman soldier. Christ entered the New Covenant by allowing His body to be cut. By His shed blood Christ gave His life and purchased His Bride which is the church. This incredible act of love depicts the seriousness of initiating a covenant with YHWH. It is also a powerful message to husbands that we should be willing to lay our lives down for our wives.

If our wives believe that we love them enough to sacrifice our lives for them that will speak volumes about our commitment. When we exchange our vows in the Covenant of Marriage that is symbolic of our 'cutting' and sealing the covenant.

YESHUA Himself ordained the Covenant of Marriage. YESHUA also honored the Covenant of Marriage by attending the wedding of a friend in Cana of Galilee in gospel of John 2:1-12. It was at this marriage that YESHUA conducted His first of many miracles that would be proof positive that He is the Messiah. Inviting YHWH Himself to be present at their wedding puts their marriage on a solid foundation from the beginning.

Covenant and Completeness

"The purpose of a man is to love a woman
And the purpose of a woman is to love a man
So, come on baby let's start today,
Come on baby let's play the game of love, la la la la love

It started long ago in the Garden of Eden
When Adam said to Eve 'baby you're for me'
["The Game of Love" by Wayne Fontana and
The Mind Benders – 1983]

Good lyrics but inaccurate theology as King Solomon 3,000 years ago challenged us with this truth:

> *"The end of the matter; all has*
> *been heard. 'Fear GOD*
> *and keep HIS commandments,*
> *for this is the whole duty*
> *of man. For GOD will bring every*
> *deed into judgement,*
> *with every secret thing, whether*
> *good or evil".*
> *[Ecclesiastes 12:13,14 – ESV]*

The song lyrics do challenge me to answer the question, "What is the purpose of marriage?" The marriage covenant was designed by YHWH with a purpose encompassed in the concept of completeness. YHWH is the Creator of the universe. His creative work was accomplished in six days. The first three days of His creative work focused on speaking into existence the life support systems – the air, the land and the water. His next three days were invested in filling those life support systems with birds, sea creatures, and land animals. The culmination of His creative work focused upon humanity. Like a potter, YHWH took dust from the ground and fashioned a human body. That body was not alive until YHWH breathed the breath of life into history's first human being named Adam. The Jewish New Year is Rosh Hashana. On Rosh Hashana Jews assemble in synagogues all over the world to blow the shofar. The blowing of the shofar represents the blowing of the breath of YHWH into Adam.

In Jewish history the current year 2021 / 2022 is the year 5782 on the Hebrew calendar. The Jews calculate that it was 5,782 years ago when YHWH created Adam.

*"One is the loneliest number
that you'll ever do..."
[Three Dog Night – 1968]*

Four Primary Purposes for Marriage

- *Pattern for Intimacy*
  - *Genesis 2:18*
- *Plentitude*
  - *Genesis 2:18*
  - *Principle of Completeness*
- *Passion*
  - *Genesis 2:24,25*
  - *I Corinthians 7*
- *Procreation*
  - *Genesis 1:28*
  - *Malachi 2:15*
- *Picture of Christ [Bridegroom] and the Church [His Bride]*
  - *Ephesians 5:22-33*

[Larry Bell ><>]

Adam was unique in all of creation. He was the only portion of creation who knew that God existed. Adam was made in the image of his Creator. Adam was intelligent, and articulate, and could choose to develop his relationship with YHWH. Adam was given the responsibility of being the first taxonomer in history. In the process of naming the animals he reached an unavoidable conclusion – he was the only human being. There were males and females of the animal kingdom, but there was no female, no counterpart, for him. Adam was alone in his humanity. Adam found himself to be incomplete in and of himself. There was no possibility of perpetuating himself and increasing the population of humans on the earth. Adam's Creator, the Great Physician, evaluated Adam's condition and declared the first diagnosis in human history:

> *"It is not good that man*
> *should be alone."*
> *[Genesis 2:18 NIV]*

YHWH developed the original treatment plan that would of necessity require Adam to undergo the initial surgical procedure in history. YHWH removed a 'rib' from the side of Adam and fashioned the perfect cure for Adam's aloneness. Adam and Eve were both incomplete in and of themselves. They entered the covenant of marriage in order to complete one another. Husbands and wives both have strengths and weaknesses. When we enter the Covenant of Marriage we need to encourage and challenge each other to accentuate our strengths and recognize our weaknesses. My wife, Deanna, has a gift of discernment in knowing when people are lying. I often defer to her and trust her judgement which is exceptionally accurate.

Adam and Eve became the first couple in human history to enter the Covenant of Marriage. Their marriage became the gold standard for all humanity. That standard is for one man and one woman to leave their biological and or their sociological situations and be totally committed to one another. This covenant model would be passed down generationally.

Men and women would 'Leave' all other relationships and be completely devoted to one another. They would continue to 'Cleave' to each other and emotionally bond. They would become 'One Flesh' and passionately celebrate their covenant love.

"Marriage is not an invention of
men, but a DIVINE institution,
and therefore, is to be religiously
observed, because it is a figure of
the inseparable union between
CHRIST and HIS church."
[Matthew Henry Commentary
on Mark 10:6]

Millions of people over the last 3500 years have followed this format
in entering the Covenant of Marriage. The word of YHWH is absolute
truth. If we are guided by His Word we then invite His very Presence
into our marriages. That is the best formula for a healthy and enduring
marriage covenant.

The most expensive weddings in
history? Possibly, the marriage of
Sheik Rashid Bin Saeed Al Makroumi's
son to Princess Salama in Dubai of
May 1981. Cost: $44,000,000!!!
According to the Guiness Book of World
Records, the "most expensive wedding
ever recorded took place in Versailles,
France in 2004, and racked up an
eye-watering $55,000,000 price tag.
The happy bride and groom were
Vanisha Mittal and Amit Bhatia.
[09/19/2020]

In 1960 there were 40,200,000 married couples in the United States. In 2020 there were 62,300,000 married couples. In the United States we still average 6,200 marriages per day or 2,300,000 per year. We spend approximately $72,000,000,000 per year on weddings and $8,000,000,000 per year on honeymoons. Clearly the wedding industry in America is big business.

In 2020 according to the National Center for Health there were 2,132,853 marriages.

We also witnessed 782,038 divorces. Our society is becoming increasingly accustomed to divorce. In 2008, the Barna Group conducted a study on marriage and divorce. The study found that 88% of the folks in America enter marriage. That study would also indicate that 12% of the population never marries. 33% of those responding to the survey questions indicated that they expected their marriage to end in divorce. George Barna made some interesting observations concerning the state of marriage in our country.

> *"Americans have grown comfortable with divorce as a normal part of life. There no longer seems to be much of a stigma attached to divorce; it is seen now as an unavoidable rite of passage. Interviews with young adults suggest they want their marriage to last, but are not particularly optimistic about that possibility. There is also evidence that many young people are moving toward embracing the idea of serial marriage, in which a person gets married two or three times seeking a different partner for each phase of their adult life.*

> *America has become an experimental, experience-driven culture. Rather than learn from objective information and teaching based on that information, people prefer to follow their instincts and let the chips fall where they may. Given that tendency we can expect*

America to retain the highest divorce rate among all developed nations In the world."

If marriages are entered into with the expectation they will not last, then failure becomes a self-fulfilling prophecy. Rather than seriously work on reconciling their marriages many folks are choosing to terminate their marriage. Another disturbing trend, as we observe an elevating divorce rate, is that there is becoming less and less of a distinction between those who believe in God and regularly attend church and those who are secular in their beliefs. This must be very disheartening to YHWH. I believe we need to change our perspectives from the beginning of entering the Covenant of Marriage.

We should still enter the marriage with the goal of longevity and 'til death do us part' commitment. That perspective places our mindset on a positive course that is in alignment with the design of our Creator. If people enter marriage anticipating a divorce it actually increases the likelihood of divorcing. The mind becomes desensitized to the necessity for long-term commitment and divorce is rationalized as the acceptable alternative.

Paul wrote to the church in Corinth, Greece:

> *"...so that no advantage would be taken*
> *of us by Satan,*
> *for we are not ignorant of his schemes."*
> *[II Corinthians 2:11 – NASB]*

Peter writes this admonition:

> *"Be soberminded, be watchful.*
> *Your adversary the devil prowls around like a roaring lion, seeking someone to devour."*
> *[I Peter 5:8 – ESV]*

It behooves us to realize the impact of spiritual warfare upon the Covenant of Marriage. This became evident in the marriage of Adam and Eve. The enemy and deceiver of mankind engaged in a conversation with Eve and convinced her to disobey the will of God.

Adam immediately followed and sin invaded humanity. The enemy seeks to 'divide and conquer'. This scheme was in evidence in the first marriage of human history and remains a threat today. Satan does not desire reconciliation of marriages. His scheme is to cause turmoil, dissension, and eventual destruction of the Covenant of Marriage. I encourage couples to be aware of this and pray individually for their marriages and together with their spouse for their marriages. Prayer is a powerful therapeutic tool. The enemy knows that YHWH instituted the Covenant of Marriage and he actively opposes the things of God.

Getting married is easy.
Staying married is more difficult.
Staying happily married for a
lifetime takes hard work.
Work hard – it's worth it!!
[TreyAndLea.com]

In a traditional exchange of vows, which is still prevalent in America, we usually promise to love, honor, and cherish each other. This promise is to be kept in good times and bad, for better or for worse, for richer or for poorer, in sickness and health; and forsaking all others. The final clause in this traditional format is: "Til death do us part". These particular clauses in the exchange of vows are compatible with the design God has for our marriages to endure.

Obviously, we have freedom and flexibility to choose the various components of the vows that we exchange in our culture. It is still essential to follow Biblical principles and expectations. Some of the wording that I have seen being utilized has the potential to jeopardize the permanent nature of the Covenant of Marriage. I've seen that some couples are concluding their marriage covenant with these words: "As long as we both shall love". This type of semantic engineering implies an 'out' clause that can be used to justify virtually any reason to disband the covenant.

In ancient Judaism Beit Hillel allowed a husband to divorce his wife for a trivial offense such as burning his evening meal!! The leading terminology that the legal profession uses in divorce proceedings is "Irreconcilable Differences". Many times, in counseling I find it is more of a refusal to reconcile than actual "irreconcilable differences".

For those of us who are Christians, I would defer to the truth that "I can do all things through Him Who strengthens me". [Philippians 4:13 – ESV] Reconciliation requires determination and work and many couples simply choose not to make a genuine effort to reconcile. YHWH is in the business of reconciliation and if that was not true, we would all find ourselves in a hopeless situation. We can choose to honor the Covenant Commitment and ask YHWH to intervene on behalf of our marriage. That paves a path for reconciliation and healing to transpire.

In South Africa, the parents of both the bride and groom traditionally carried fire from the hearths of their homes to the house of the newlyweds. The fire from both parents' homes is then used to ignite a new fire in the home of the married couple.
[Credit: 'the knot" website]

Commitment is what is described in Genesis 2:24,25 as 'leave'. The English word leave comes from the Hebrew word 'azab'. The Hebrew patriarch Jacob experienced a dream through which YHWH would speak to him. He saw a ladder extending from earth to heaven and the LORD stood above it. God spoke these words to Jacob:

> *"Behold, I am with you and*
> *will keep you wherever you go,*
> *and will bring you back to this land.*
> *For I will not 'leave' you…"*
> *[Genesis 28:15 – ESV]*

YHWH would honor His word to Jacob and his name was eventually changed to Israel. Jacob and his descendants would be established in the land of Israel. Jacob was realizing his inclusion in the covenant YHWH made with his grandfather Abraham in Genesis 12:1-3. YHWH promised HE would not leave Jacob and that He would fulfill His covenantal promise. This is the same perspective that is necessary in entering into the marriage covenant. Marriage can endure if we maintain an unwavering determination to fulfill the vows that we have exchanged.

This is accentuated by our LORD when He said:

> *"I will never leave you nor*
> *forsake you. So, we can confidently*
> *say, 'The LORD is my helper; I will*
> *not fear, what can man do to me?'"*
> *[Hebrews 13:5,6 – ESV]*

YESHUA will never leave or forsake those who have chosen to follow Him. This is a deliberate and willful choice that He has made and will not change. We can trust Him and His promise. That is the type of determination we need to exhibit toward our spouse when we exchange vows.

In our culture we often associate the marriage covenant with being 'in love'.

I have been in the counseling profession for over four decades, I have had the opportunity to work with hundreds of couples in marital counseling. Numerous times I have heard one spouse or the other indicate they want a divorce because they 'feel' they don't 'love' their spouse anymore. Love is a deliberate and willful choice. The Hebrew words used for the love of GOD in the Original Testament refer to 'total loyalty' or 'unfailing love'. When we enter the Covenant of Marriage we should be committed to that type of love. True love will honor the covenant commitment. YHWH has created and programmed us with the ability to experience and express a wide range of feelings. Feelings are important, but should not be the primary determinative factor in disbanding the covenant of marriage. It seems some people prioritize their feelings in order to rationalize their decision to divorce.

Other relationships that we have change to some degree when we enter the marriage covenant. We need to leave the home of our family of origin and establish our own household. We still need to love and honor our parents as we begin living our lives separated from them. Relationships with other family members also are subject to change as we prioritize the place of our spouse in our marriage.

Queen Victoria's wedding cake
weighed 300 pounds.
I guess she let them 'eat cake'!!!

The Hebrew word for "leave' is directly related to the unwavering commitment needed in sustaining our marriages. We leave our biological and or sociological situations to enter into the Covenant of Marriage and we should place our spouse in a position of priority. The husband should treat his wife as the most important woman on planet earth. The wife should treat her husband as the most important man on the planet. If we can realize this perspective, there is a reciprocity established that will bond the relationship firmly. The couple puts themselves on a unique 'step' and from a human standpoint no one else is on that step. There is a sense of completeness and absolute exclusivity that promotes the well-being of each other that must be attained.

I have observed on multiple occasions that there are in fact 'in-law' problems. For example I remember one husband who really never 'left and cleft'. His mother was continually attempting to put herself on equal footing with his wife. In fact, this mother was placing herself in authority over him and his wife. His mother attempted to control many things in their marriage such as the holiday visitation schedule. His mother expected them to be present with her every Thanksgiving, Christmas, Easter and at Independence Day cookouts. She would become very upset if her son wanted to spend time with his wife's family during those times. This became a huge problem due to the husband's unwillingness to establish appropriate boundaries and prioritize his wife. His insensitivity to this situation caused major turmoil. His wife became extremely frustrated to the point she believed she was in competition with her mother-in-law for her husband's love and attention. This husband had to realize how this was being perceived by his wife and take appropriate measures to ensure equitable investment of time with both families. Over time he was able to adjust his mindset and behavior and the conflict became resolved. Our perspectives become our reality and if our perspective is accurate it needs validation from our spouse. It has been my observation that husbands have more difficulty in validating the perspectives of their wives than vice versa.

*"You're my soul and my heart's
inspiration
You're all I got to get me by
You're my soul and my heart's
inspiration
Without you baby what good am I?
Oh, what good am I?"
[Righteous Brothers – 1966]*

I have witnessed situations where the husband wants to lead a single lifestyle in the context of a marriage. He still desired to invest extraordinary amounts of time with his friends playing sports and socializing without including his wife. Another husband I've worked with expected his wife to be on board with him using the entirety of his vacation time for hunting ventures and not use any of that time to be with his bride. We all need friends, but friendships should not be detrimental to the marriage.

Clyde and Cathy [not their real names] began having marital problems after a couple of years. The biggest issue was that Cathy began to feel uncomfortable about the relationship that Clyde had developed with Brenda. Clyde and Cathy were both friends with Brenda and her husband, Jeff. They did a few things together as couples, but then Clyde and Brenda started sharing time and activities together without Cathy and Jeff. They would go to lunch together, jog together, and talk and text an inordinate amount of time. When Cathy brought this to Clyde's attention, he would just scoff at her and shrug it off. Cathy was feeling disrespected and threatened. Clyde refused to validate her feelings or make any genuine attempt to understand her viewpoint. The final straw came one Friday when Clyde, Cathy, and Brenda went to dinner together. After dinner Brenda came back to their house. It was already late and Cathy did not want Brenda to come over, but Clyde insisted. The three of them watched a portion of a movie together and then Cathy had to retire to bed because of commitments early on Saturday. Clyde and Brenda watched the remainder of the movie together. Cathy was awakened around 2:00 a.m. and went downstairs. Clyde and Brenda were watching yet another movie together. It was a highly stressful confrontation and Clyde resisted the idea to have Brenda leave. Clyde refused to acknowledge that this type of behavior was legitimately disconcerting to Cathy. Cathy was able to get Clyde to come to a couple of counseling sessions. He finally discontinued his participation in counseling because he adamantly did not want to change his behavior. He did not want to impair his relationship with Brenda and expected Cathy to just leave well enough alone. There are 'red flags' abounding the inappropriate relationship that has developed between Clyde and Brenda.

Cathy decided to come for counseling individually and worked out what she felt were acceptable boundaries and expectations for Clyde and Brenda. She became resolved in her determination and developed an ultimatum. Currently, Cathy continues in counseling awaiting Clyde's response. It is my opinion that Clyde is 'not forsaking all others'. He is not honoring his wife and placing her in the position of priority that she deserves. His self-centeredness and unwillingness to change may eventually cost him his marriage.

*"FOR SALE: 1994 Mercedes –
240 SL – Loaded.
First fifty dollars takes it.
868-5737"
Not believing his eyes, a man
called the number to see if the
"fifty dollars" was a misprint.
The woman assured him it wasn't.
She was indeed selling the car*

*for fifty dollars, and there was
absolutely nothing wrong with it.
The man rushed to her home,
gave her fifty dollars cash, and she
handed him the title to the luxurious
automobile. He asked the obvious
question: "Why are you selling a
Mercedes for fifty dollars?"
"Well, my husband phoned me
from Las Vegas. He's there with
his secretary, and said he's leaving
me. He went broke gambling and he
asked me to sell the Mercedes and send
him half of what I get for it."
[Appeared in Dear Abby]*

After we enter the marriage covenant, we must be willing to modify our relational priorities with others in such a way that our spouse senses that we value them above all others. This will accentuate that we honor our spouse. This perspective will help us to follow the principle of 'Leave' as put forth in Genesis.

*In Egypt, the family of the bride
traditionally does all the cooking
for a week after the wedding, so
the couple can relax.
[Credit: 'the knot' website]*

Almost everyone experiences some positive and some negative aspects associated with their family of origin. The challenge is to be aware of

the positive and perpetuate those behaviors and to choose not to be held captive to the negative behaviors. It is an awesome blessing and responsibility to welcome children into our families. Our children are being programmed by us as parents. Sons are likely to imitate the behaviors learned from their fathers. Sons are quite likely to be the kind of husband and dad that their father was when they were growing up. Daughters will likely be the kind of wife and mother as their own mother. Moses writes these words:

> *"Hear O Israel the LORD our GOD, the LORD is ONE. Love the LORD your GOD with all your heart and with all your soul and with all your strength. These commandments that I give you today are to be on your hearts. Impress them on your children. Talk about them when you sit at home and when you walk along the road, when you lie down and when you get up. Tie them as symbols on your hands and bind them on your foreheads. Write them on the doorframes of your house and on your gates."* *[Deuteronomy 6:4-6 - NIV]*

In the Original Testament this section of scripture is called "The Shema". This is one of the very most important sections in all of the Original Testament. Shema literally means 'to hear'. When YHWH spoke to Moses at the tabernacle His Shekinah glory hovered over the Holy of Holies. The Hebrew phrase "Holy of Holies" literally means 'to speak'. YHWH directly spoke to Moses there. YHWH has something to say to us and our responsibility is to listen, learn and obey. The text above demonstrates the importance of taking every opportunity to instruct our children in the way that is pleasing to God. We are to talk about the truth of God's Word and then lead by example. It is a fact that family of origin behaviors are typically transmitted to the next generation. It behooves us to pray and seek to be the very best husband or wife possible. It is important to instruct our children. It is equally important to model appropriate behaviors to our children. Modeling is a powerful type of teaching and undoubtedly the most impactful. If we say one thing and do the opposite, we demonstrate a lack of integrity. If I verbalized a profanity as a teenager, Dad would be quick to point that out and discipline me for it [rightfully so!]. But if I pointed out the fact that he used that same language I could expect this response: "Do as I say, not as I do". If our behavior matches our words then we have demonstrated a walk of integrity. That is pleasing in the sight of YHWH if we are following His principles. Modeling a healthy marriage brings honor to our Creator and can be imparted and perpetuated to the next generations.

I was raised in the rural community of Elkins, West Virginia. In my home my parents were committed to one another and ended up being married for 50 years until my father passed away in 1996. Like any marriage they experienced their struggles in raising four boys.

Both of my parents worked hard to provide for us. I rarely saw either of them relaxing as there was always something to do. They taught me the importance of work and developing a good work ethic. They challenged all four of us to do well academically. Even though they 'bickered' a lot they stayed the course and achieved an enduring commitment to each other in the Covenant of Marriage. Their obvious commitment to the Covenant of Marriage was something especially positive and my desire was to have that type of commitment to my bride.

My mother was born and raised in Texas. She had always pressured us in a positive way to do well academically because she was the Salutatorian of her class in Texas. You can imagine that we heard about that recognition on multiple occasions. In 1996 my mother returned to Texas for her 55th High School Reunion. She was awarded the prize for coming the farthest as she resided in Maryland at the time. She had a wonderful time catching up with her classmates and visiting her hometown. When she returned she showed me a picture of those attending the reunion. There were only nine people in the picture. I responded to her "Wow!! You must have lost a lot of classmates". She then informed me that they had only lost one in her graduating class!! So, Katye Ruth Sheffield Bell was the Salutatorian of Penelope High School in Penelope, Texas with a graduating class of ten people!! Penelope is 20 miles south of Ft. Worth and even today only boasts a population of approximately 200 people. My brothers and I had just assumed everything was big in Texas and she told us no differently. I often teased her that there must have been one Valedictorian and nine Salutatorians! It was because of my mother's example and encouragement that I was motivated to complete two university degrees. I now appreciate her example and am grateful for her encouragement.

None of us are perfect. My mother was not perfect. She loved and nurtured me, and I have many positive memories of her. One flaw in her character was being a grudge holder.

When my mother became angry with someone it was difficult for her to resolve that issue in a constructive manner. She would frequently allow her anger to turn into resentment.

Unresolved anger and resentment eventually transform into bitterness. When bitterness takes root in the life of a person the consequences can be injurious. Her bitterness sometimes was expressed in a vengeful spirit.

*"My most brilliant achievement was my ability to be able to persuade my wife to marry me.
[Sir Winston Churchill]*

My mother and I had a good relationship overall. In 1991 things changed after I returned from a mission trip to Estonia and Russia. I was interviewed on television about my trip and the interviewer asked me when I became a Christian. I remember very clearly how I responded. I

informed him that my parents did the right thing by taking me to church every Sunday. However, I did not become a Christian, a true follower of CHRIST, until I was 25 years old. The problem was with my heart and my parents were not to blame for my spiritual condition. After that initial question, the interview centered around the experiences I had while on the mission trip. The interviewer sent me a videotape of my thirty-minute interview.

I gave the video to my parents to view when they had come to visit us. We were busy preparing the Thanksgiving meal and I had even forgotten they had taken time to watch the video. Later that evening I recalled they had viewed the video and thought it was odd that neither of them offered a response to me. A couple of days later I received a scathing letter from my mother.

She had grossly misunderstood and misconstrued my comments about when I actually became a Christian. I attempted to explain what I clearly meant, and she absolutely refused to listen. In fact, it got to the point where she did not want to discuss it at all. This incident occurred in 1991. From that time on I would continue to visit my mom, talk with her regularly on the phone and even provide some financial support on occasion. Over the years I had convinced myself that she had put this matter completely behind her. When she passed away on August 22, 2012, I quickly realized that was an inaccurate assumption. She completely wrote me out of her last will and testament. She chose to be consumed with that bitterness for twenty-one years!!! She consulted with a lawyer to prepare her will. The lawyer advised her to leave me something or I might be able to contest the will. My mother bequeathed a two-dollar bill to me!!! I was obviously hurt and disappointed but most of all perplexed. I decided to learn from that negative characteristic in her life in such a way that I would not pass it on to my children. My mother lived to be eighty-eight years of age. Perhaps she would have become of centenarian if she had not allowed bitterness to control her. I prayerfully chose to forgive my mother and not allow the seed of bitterness to consume my life.

I share this because I had a choice. I chose to replicate the academic encouragement that I had received from my mother by encouraging my children to excel academically.

I made a deliberate choice to not allow bitterness to ruin my life. I was resolute in not passing the root of bitterness to the next generation of the Bell clan.

Punctuation is Powerful
An English professor wrote the words:
"A woman without her man is nothing"
on the whiteboard, and he asked his
students to punctuate it correctly.
All the males in the class wrote:
"A woman, without her man, is nothing."
All the females in the class wrote:
"A woman: without her, man is nothing!"
[Meme on Facebook – August 20, 2021 –
no author cited]

I learned from a marriage that lasted 50 years to be undeterred in my marriage covenant. My wife and I have now been married for 48 years. My wife and I were fortunate to have excellent role models with her parents who also honored their Covenant of Marriage for more than 50 years. I am thankful to my parents that they remained committed to the Covenant of Marriage despite the trials they experienced. The latter years of their marriage certainly tested their resolve and they remained undeterred in their commitment to the Covenant of Marriage. That is a

commitment that was passed down to me and I intend to honor and per-petuate that type of commitment.

Juno, the Roman goddess, ruled over marriage, the hearth, and childbirth. This has probably contributed to the popularity of June weddings in the Western World.
[Credit: "the knot" website]

Up to this point I have discussed the concept of "Leave" that is also encap-sulated as Commitment. I am going to transition at this juncture to con-nect the Greek word 'agape' to the expectations encompassed in 'Leave' and 'Commitment'. In many weddings couples select the following pas-sage to be read:

"Love is patient and kind;
love does not envy or boast;
it is not arrogant or rude.
It does not insist on its own way.
It is not irritable or resentful;
it does not rejoice at wrongdoing,
but rejoices with the truth.
Love bears all things, believes
all things, hopes all thing, endures
all things. Love never ends."
[I Corinthians 13:4-8 – NIV]

Every time you see the English word 'love' in this section of scripture it is derived from the Greek word 'agapao' or 'agape'. Meaningful definitions of 'agape' love are provided in the NIV and Strong's concordance. Agape is an unconditional love or unfailing love. Agape is a love that is unconcerned about self and is primarily demonstrates concern for the other person. Agape is a deliberate and willful choice. Agape love is exemplified and personified in in the Gospel of John which is probably the most quoted verse in the entire New Testament:

> *"For God so loved the world that*
> *He gave His only begotten Son,*
> *that whosoever believeth in Him*
> *should not perish, but have*
> *everlasting life."*
> *[John 3:16 -KJV]*

The love of God, demonstrated in His willingness to offer Himself as a sacrifice for our sins, is the most perfect expression of agape. Agape is a self-sacrificing love that puts the other person, and their needs, in the place of priority. Humanity owed a debt due to sin that we could not pay. YHWH paid our debt when YESHUA sacrificed Himself at Calvary.

> *"The great marriages are*
> *partnerships. It can't be a*
> *great marriage without being*
> *a partnership."*
> *[Helen Mirren]*

When you read I Corinthians 13:4-8 there is no notation that states: "Use this in marriages". This is a portion of the letter that Paul wrote to followers of "The Way" in Corinth, Greece. This should be the way we strive to treat believers in the church. It is also particularly applicable to the Covenant of Marriage. If both the husband and wife aspire to this level

of love their marriage can pass the test of time. The principle of reciprocity is essential. It is a complete covenant if both husband and wife share the 'agape' perspective.

Agape love can be further expressed in these types of mental determinations:

> ➤ *"I promise to love my spouse because I made a commitment in the sight of GOD to love my spouse".*

> ➤ *"I promise to love my spouse because it's my choice to do the right thing".*

> ➤ *"I promise to love my spouse in such a way to give them every support, encouragement and challenge to be the best spouse they can be. And I promise to model that behavior by being the best spouse I can be".*

> ➤ *"I promise to love my spouse although they are not perfect,*

realizing that I am not perfect either".

My contention is that we must make this type of mental mindset transform into a behavioral reality. If we can accomplish this type of love, which is unconditional, then "Irreconcilable Differences" can become 'Reconcilable'. Agape love intensifies our commitment to our spouses. Agape love challenges us to be more like YESHUA.

*In 1104 A.D. a Prior in a small town in
Essex, England had an audience with a
local Lord and his wife. He was unaware
because the couple was disguised as
'commoners'. They asked for a blessing
from the Prior because they had not
argued for one year of being married.
The Prior was impressed with their devotion
and presented them with a 'flitch' – which
is a side of bacon. The Lord and Lady
revealed their true identities. They awarded
the monastery additional land under the
condition that the Prior would award the
'flitch' to couples who demonstrated similar
devotion. Contestants would come from far
and wide to enter the contest. The contest
is called the Dunmow Flitch and is still held
every four years. This is where the term,
"Bring home the bacon" originated.
[Origin of the Phrase "Bring Home the
Bacon" // JonathanBecher.com / 06/14/2020]*

Divorce Considerations

*A priest offers sacrifices on behalf of the people to GOD. A prophet speaks
on behalf of God to the people. The last book included in the Original
Testament was written by the prophet Malachi in the 5th century B.C.
Malachi gives us these words concerning God's opinion concerning divorce:*

"The man who hates and divorces
his wife, says the LORD,
the God of Israel, does violence
to the one he should protect,
says the LORD Almighty."
[Malachi 2:16 – NIV]

"For the LORD GOD of Israel
says that He hates divorce..."
[Malachi 2:16 – NKJV]

It is quite apparent that YHWH hates divorce. Being in the counseling business I get a glimpse into the mind of God and why He has recorded this stern point of view. Divorce always causes bleak consequences regardless of the reason for the divorce. Divorce is always difficult on the husband and wife. If the couple has children, divorce always impacts them nega-tively and can cause severe psychological turmoil in their lives. I am con-tinually amazed by parents who are on a collision course for divorce and demonstrate almost a 'carefree' attitude towards the effect this decision will have on their children.

When marital difficulties become evident, effort should be heavily invested in restoration. YHWH is in the business of reconciliation, and HE provides us a great source of strength if we rely upon Him. We need to pray for our spouse and with our spouse. We need to study the scriptures and ask the Holy Spirit to lead us into truth and apply that truth to our marriage. We can also request that HE empower us to be a peacemaker. Paul wrote to the church at Rome:

"If possible, so far as it
depends on you,
live peaceably with all".
[Romans 12:18 – ESV]

In the Sermon on the Mount overlooking the Sea of Galilee YESHUA taught His disciples:

> *"Blessed are the peacemakers*
> *for they shall be called*
> *sons of God".*
> *[Matthew 5:9 – ESV]*

Both spouses can choose to embrace the concept of personally being a peacemaker.

If they develop this mindset then they can begin to focus on what they can do to make things better. This will require introspection into what they have done to contribute to the difficulties in their marriage. And then they can prayerfully pursue what changes are necessary for improving their relationship with their spouse.

I have never met one couple where the husband was 100% at fault in causing marital difficulties and the wife was zero percent wrong or vice versa. In 2002 I received a call from a lady wanting to schedule an appointment for her and her husband. My office had a window which faced the parking lot and I could observe clients coming into the building. This lady was figuratively almost dragging her husband into the session. She was walking with intention and had a stern look of disgust on her face. I normally have the couple sit down and get some preliminary background information. But this lady was completely fed-up with her husband and could not wait to get started. She interrupted me and looked at her husband as her nostrils flared and said: "Tell him what you've done!!!" He proceeded to admit to me several offenses that he had committed. I acknowledged that I understood what had transpired and how hurtful those things were to his wife. After a couple of minutes, I decided to temper the situation somewhat and indicated that no one in the room, including myself, was perfect. I proceeded to say that in a marriage that is having trouble, I usually find that there is something positive both parties can do to improve their marriage. This lady was absolutely incensed that I had spoken those words. She informed me that her husband was completely to blame '100%', followed by an expletive! She proceeded to exit the office and refused to return.

Her husband and I spoke briefly for a couple of minutes, and he joined her in the car. She would not 'allow' him to come back on his own for counseling and vehemently refused any further attempts at marital counseling with me. A couple of weeks later I went to eat lunch at our local Panera Bread restaurant. After I ordered and received my food, I walked down an aisle to an open table. That lady was sitting about three tables away. When she saw me, she very quickly wrapped up her food and exited stage right! Thankfully, that is the only time I have had that type of experience. I hope that couple eventually received the counseling assistance they badly needed. I suspect that counseling of a genuinely therapeutic nature would not transpire until she dealt with her arrogant attitude.

"An archaeologist is the best husband a woman can have. The older she gets, the more interested he is in her."
[Agatha Christie]

In 1995 my parents were impacted by a severe set of trials and tribulations. My father had been battling depression for several years. He was being treated successfully by appropriate medication. For some reason, still unknown to me, his physician decided to change his medication to a new experimental drug. One of the harmful side effects listed on the label was the potential for a hypo-manic break. Unfortunately, my father experienced a severe hypo-manic break. He would stay awake for days

on end. He would talk rapidly and incessantly. He began hitch-hiking around in the dead of winter with only a windbreaker. He was on the run from his family. He was smart enough to elude us for months. Eventually, my brothers and I found out his location and made him go with us to the hospital. I was driving my mother's car to transport him to obtain appropriate medical attention. While we were discussing his condition with the doctor he excused himself to go to the bathroom. He was taking an extraordinary amount of time. I went to check on him and he was gone. He had an extra key to the car in his billfold and left us at the hospital 15 miles from the house. He finally ended up getting an apartment in my hometown of Elkins, WV. He was contacted by mental health professionals and eventually stabilized. He was absent from home for almost a year. It appeared on several occasions that my parents' marriage would end in divorce. The thought of that kept me disturbed greatly and I was forty-five years old. I personally observed my parents successfully endure this season of trial. Their commitment to one another remained intact through this stressful time. They were fully aware of the 'good times and bad', 'for better or worse', and 'in sickness and in health' components of the vows they exchanged. Their commitment to the Covenant of Marriage was highly impactful in my life. I can understand how injurious a divorce can be to a young child when it was overwhelming to me as a forty-five-year-old man.

*"Marriage is not a noun;
it's a verb. It is not something
you get. It's something you do.
It's the way you love your partner
everyday."
[Barbara DeAngelis]*

In the scripture these three specific sections address the topic of divorce.

Deuteronomy 24:1; Matthew 19:3-9 and I Corinthians 7:12-15.

Moses writes:

> *"When a man takes a wife*
> *and marries her, if then she*
> *finds no favor in his eyes because*
> *he has found some indecency*
> *[uncleanness] in her, and he writes*
> *her a certificate of divorce and puts*
> *it in her hand and sends her out of*
> *his house..."*
> *[Deuteronomy 24:1 – ESV]*

When studying about this verse in rabbinic literature there are two basic schools of thought. Rabbi Shammai was born in 50 BC. and died in 30 AD., coinciding with the onset of the public ministry of YESHUA. Rabbi Shammai was a prominent contributor to the Mishnah which is the book in which he wrote down the oral traditions of the Jews, sometimes referred to as the Oral Torah.

Rabbi Hillel 'The Elder' was traditionally believed to have been born in Babylon in 110 B.C. and died in Jerusalem in 10 A.D. His life spanned the course of 120 years which earned him the title of 'The Elder'. Rabbi Hillel contributed greatly to the writing down of the Oral Torah in the Mishnah. He also contributed to writing in the Talmud and established the House of Hillel school in Jerusalem. [Wikipedia] On a side note – Rabbi Gamaliel, grandson of Hillel, is mentioned in Acts 5. The Apostle Paul was likely a Rabbinic student of Gamaliel.

Both Rabbi Shammai and Hillel were instrumental in the formation of the ancient Jewish sect known as the Pharisees. The Sadducees only believed that the first five books of the Original Testament were to be followed. The Pharisees believed in the validity of the Torah and other sections of the Original Testament and the Oral Traditions. The Pharisees were often at odds with the teachings of YESHUA. By the time that YESHUA initiated His public ministry, the teachings of the School of Hillel were given authoritative prominence.

So, what did Moses mean when he wrote the word 'uncleanness' and what did that infer about divorce? The school of Rabbi Shammai supported the premise that indecency or uncleanness referred specifically to sexual immorality.

On the other hand, the school of Rabbi Hillel said uncleanness could encompass any type of indiscretion like ruining the breakfast of her husband. A husband could divorce his wife if she went around the house with unbound hair or talked to other men in public. Those who adhered to this line of reasoning are simply biased chauvinists. Rabbis had popularized various sayings regarding wives. "The man with a bad wife would never face hell, because he has paid for his sins on earth". "The man who is ruled by his wife has a life that is not a life".

"A bad wife is like leprosy to her husband, and the only way he could be cured is by divorce".

These thoughts present a picture of a wife being a possession more than a life partner designed to complete her husband and the husband by design completes his wife. They must not have invested much time in studying the words of Solomon in Proverbs 18:22: "He who finds a wife finds a good thing. And obtains favor from the LORD." {NKJV}

[Enduring Word Commentary, David Guzik, on google.com]

Matthew pens these words of our LORD:

"And the Pharisees came up to HIM and tested HIM by asking, "Is it lawful to divorce one's wife for any cause?' HE answered "Have you not read that HE WHO created them from the beginning made them male and female, and said, "Therefore a man shall leave his father and his mother and hold fast to his wife, and the two shall become one flesh"? So, they are no longer two but one flesh. "What therefore, God has joined together, let not man separate. They said to Him, "Why then did Moses command one to give a certificate of divorce and to send her away"? He said to them, "Because of your hardness of heart Moses allowed you to divorce your wives, but from the beginning it was not so. And I say to you, whoever divorces his wife, except for sexual immorality, and marries another, commits adultery". [Matthew 19:3-9]

It seems abundantly clear to me that Rabbi YESHUA brought clarity to this debate and obviously connected uncleanness to sexual immorality. This seems to be congruent with the Hebrew word for uncleanness in Deuteronomy 24:1. I remember having the opportunity to see the Broadway Musical 'Cats' in 2002. The oldest of the cats portrayed was named – 'Deuteronomy'- who had been around for a very long time. Like Deuteronomy, sexual immorality has been around since shortly after the dawn of humanity. It appears that YESHUA was chastising those Pharisees connected to the Rabbinic School of Hillel who were very liberal in their interpretations for granting a Certificate of Divorce. YESHUA was straightforward and focused this teaching on divorces being allowed in the case of adultery.

Adultery is a major factor that contributes to divorce in our culture. We are inundated with adultery being portrayed as the 'norm' on the movie screen and on television. It is difficult to view any shows during the primetime hours that do not glamorize sexual immorality.

Adultery is a consistent temptation that continues to devour the Covenant of Marriage.

The American Association for Marriage and Family Therapy conducts national surveys.

The results of these surveys indicate that 25% of married men have had extramarital affairs.

The survey also indicates that 15% of women have cheated on their husbands. They offer a footnote to these statistics that 'this incidence rate is about 20% higher when emotional and sexual relationships without intercourse are included'. I personally believe that if people responded with absolute confidence of anonymity that these statistics would be higher.

Moroccan women take a milk bath
to purify themselves before their
wedding ceremony.
[Credit: 'the knot' website]
Reminds me of the 1986 commercial:
"Milk: It does a body good"!!!

I will utilize the example of a hypothetical married couple. Both husband and wife are Christians. The husband succumbs to lustful temptation and becomes involved in adultery.

This husband is the 'offending party', and his wife is the 'offended party'. When she becomes aware of the unfaithfulness of her husband, she is devastated emotionally. Trust is completely demolished. They both have major decisions to make. She is deciding whether she should reconcile. He may be considering whether he wants to be with the other woman. Over time he decides to admit that he is wrong and asks his wife to forgive him and then restore the marriage. Christians have been forgiven and as a result she will need to forgive him. Paul expounded upon forgiveness in his letter to the Ephesians:

"Be kind to one another, tenderhearted, forgiving one another, as GOD in CHRIST forgave you".
[Ephesians 4:32 – ESV]

Forgiving her adulterous husband does not automatically result in the reconciliation of the marriage. If she chooses to forgive and desires reconciliation that can only be achieved via a significant amount of counseling and time for the husband to prove that he is genuine.

Trust takes a significant amount of time to be established in a marriage and only a few moments of sexual immorality to be destroyed. It seems to me that the wife could forgive her husband but not choose to reconcile the marriage because of the emotional trauma that she has experienced.

"A good marriage is the union of two good forgivers."
[Ruth Bell Graham]

My primary approach in marriage counseling is to facilitate reconciliation. In 2007 I began working with a couple whose marriage was on the verge of collapse. The wife did not trust the husband. The husband persisted in his stance that he had not been and was not being unfaithful to his wife. He maintained this stance even when he filed for divorce. I happened to be going to watch the West Virginia University football team play against the University of Maryland at the stadium in College Park, MD. It was about a four-hour drive from my home. My wife and two

friends traveled with me. Our son was coming from Lynchburg, Virginia and I had to wait outside of the stadium in order to give him his ticket. A huge crowd was entering into the stadium. I was standing amid this crowd when a couple emerged from the crowd and was standing right in front of me. It was the man who had been denying all along that he was not being unfaithful to his wife. I have the look on his face indelibly etched in my memory bank. I was immediately able to contact his wife and share with her that she had been right all along. During the divorce proceedings he was forced to admit to being unfaithful. This proved very beneficial to his wife in the mind of the judge. What are the odds of this encounter being completely random and coincidental? BTW, WVU beat Maryland 31-14. Running back Noel Devine solidified himself as a starter by gaining 136 yards on five carries.

Ziona, AKA - Chana Pawl, was part of a 'Christian' polygamy-practicing sect in Mizoram, India. He held the title of being the head of the 'world's largest existing family'. He was born on July 21, 1945, and died on June 13, 2021. He had 39 wives and 94 children. {Wikipedia and Instagram July 2021}

King Solomon is still the winner with 700 wives And 300 concubines... Solomon came to this conclusion: "It is better to live in a corner of the housetop [roof] than in a house shared with a quarrelsome wife [Proverbs 25:24 – ESV]. I think Solomon spent a significant amount of time on the roof!!!

Adultery is always exposed eventually. It may take years, but the truth comes out of the darkness and moves into the light. I worked with a woman about 14 years ago. She shared with me an incredible account of how she discovered that her husband was being unfaithful.

She had been suspicious of her husband for about two years. She checked his computer and his cell phone regularly and could not find anything of an incriminating nature. She still had this 'heaviness of heart' that was persistent. She kept praying for a resolution to this emotional turmoil. One evening after work she and her husband enjoyed a meal that she had prepared. He informed her that he needed to go to the store and pick up some building supplies. He indicated that he would return in a couple of hours. His dog would accompany him on this venture. His dog would prove to be "Woman's Best Friend". He picked up his girlfriend and headed to a remote location. He was enjoying himself so much that he lost track of time. He called his wife on his cell phone and lied to her about the loading of the supplies being delayed and he would be out for another hour. He hung up and she heard the dial tone indicating they were disconnected. Her husband tossed his cell phone on the back seat while he and his girlfriend became sexually involved. All this activity caused his dog to walk back and forth and jump around. The dog stepped on his cell phone and a paw hit 'redial'. His wife's phone rang and she heard the entirety of their interaction and then hung up. When he arrived home she confronted him immediately. He denied and lied until she informed him about the cell phone call. He finally admitted the adultery to her. She then asked him how long he had been involved with this woman and he replied – "two years". Her suspicions were then validated and her marriage was subsequently terminated. She is the best example I've known personally that exemplifies the truth contained in the Book of Numbers:

"…you have sinned against the LORD and be sure your sin will find you out".
[Numbers 32:23 – ESV]

58

The Apostle Paul admonishes us with this counsel:

> *"Flee from sexual immorality!!*
> *Every other sin a person commits*
> *is outside the body, but the sexually*
> *immoral person sins against his own*
> *body. Or do you not know that your*
> *body is a temple of the Holy Spirit*
> *within you, whom you have from GOD?*
> *You are not your own, for you were bought*
> *with a price. So, glorify God in your body".*
> *[I Corinthians 6:18-20]*

Sexual immorality is highly detrimental to any marriage and is prevalent in significant numbers in our society. It is not impossible to reconcile after adultery, but it takes a major effort and an exceeding amount of grace and mercy exhibited by the offended party. I have seen couples restore their marriage after adultery. I even had one couple who had experienced the heartbreak of adultery and they divorced. Years later they came to see me for counseling and God worked in an incredible way. They healed from the adultery, reconciled their differences and they remarried. The LORD then blessed them with two beautiful children.

Pricilla Pressley's diamond engagement
Ring was a whopping 3.5 carat rock
surrounded by a detachable row of diamonds.
[Elvis must have loved her 'tender
and true'!!]

Another scripture that deals with divorce is in Paul's letter to the believers in Corinth:

"...if any brother has a wife
who is an unbeliever, and she
consents to live with him, he
should not divorce her. If any
woman has a husband who is
an unbeliever, and he consents
to live with her, she should not
divorce him.
For the unbelieving husband is
made holy because of his wife,
and the unbelieving wife is made
holy because of her husband.
Otherwise, your children would
be unclean, but as it is, they are holy.
But if the unbelieving partner
separates let it be so. In such cases
the brother or sister is not enslaved.
God has called you to peace.
For how do you know, wife, whether
you will save your husband? Or how
do you know, husband, whether you
will save your wife?
[I Corinthians 7:12-16 – ESV]

In Acts 18 we read the account of Paul, Silas and Timothy being used by YHWH to bring the gospel of Christ to Corinth. Paul's strategy in evangelization was to go to his fellow Jews and make a deliberate effort to convince them that YESHUA is the Messiah.

After that he often turned his attention to reaching the 'goim' or gentiles.

I do not pretend to know what exactly caused Paul to write the counsel included in the text quoted above. Let's assume this hypothetical situation.

Paul, Timothy, and Silas invited the townspeople of Corinth to a scriptural presentation that would be held in the theater. The actual remains of a theater have been discovered archaeologically in Corinth and I had the opportunity to see these ruins in 2001. Let's further imagine that several curious folks accepted the invitation and came to the theater. Paul addressed the crowd and explained who YESHUA is and what HE had accomplished for them. He made it clear that he believed that YESHUA was in fact the long-awaited Messiah. Then Paul provided them the invitation to ask YESHUA to forgive them of their sins, come into their lives, and be born again. You can imagine the various reactions and some may have left when Paul presented the facts of the resurrection. But there was one God fearing woman who believed the truth and she called upon YESHUA and was genuinely converted. She and her husband had both been present, but he was non-responsive. When they returned home, she wanted to meet with the other believers for corporate worship and study. She volunteered for projects to assist those in poverty. She even wanted to take some of their family income and support the mission team.

After a few months of observing the changes in her life, her husband becomes frustrated with her. He decides to leave her because of her faith and the fact she was a disciple of YESHUA.

This is a possible scenario why Paul included this section in his epistle to Corinth. The believing woman was to stay in the marriage in hopes of converting her unbelieving husband. When he decided to leave, because of her faith, she was no longer bound in marriage.

I have seen some folks attempt an interesting application of this section of scripture.

I know a Christian lady who dated and eventually married a non-Christian. After years of frustration, she attempted to use these verses as justification to end her marriage.

That is just not compatible with the situation outlined by Paul. In Corinth the husband and wife came to the theater, and neither were believers. The husband chose to leave because of the newly found faith of his wife. Going into a marriage already knowing her husband is not a Christian and then trying to apply this 'non-believing spouse clause' would be a misapplication of the intent of Paul's teaching.

"Marriage is not an invention of men, but a divine institution, and therefore is to be religiously observed, because it is a figure of the inseparable union between CHRIST and HIS church."
[Matthew Henry Commentary on Mark 10:6]

Over the centuries Rabbinic teachings have evolved. Many Rabbis are excellent authorities on applying the principles contained in the Original Testament. I will summarize some of the rabbinical teaching concerning divorce. Many rabbinical scholars propose three reasons for a divorce to be granted: Adultery, Abuse and Abandonment.

We have already studied the case for adultery. What about abuse?

There are basically two types of abuse – physical and emotional. Physical abuse is always accompanied by emotional abuse. Emotional abuse does not always find expression in physical abuse. It is an absolute fact that physical and emotional abuse are both traumatic and should not be tol-erated in a marriage. The preponderance of physical abuse is perpetrated by the husband. How does this relate to divorce? I am confident in saying that GOD does not desire a wife to be physically or emotionally abused. I have been involved in situations in which the wife was living in constant fear and turmoil. I have assisted women in leaving their homes and even going in hiding. There are domestic violence centers in most communi-ties that are invaluable in providing assistance. I believe that the wife who has been living in an abusive relationship should become involved in counseling in order to tend to her physical and emotional health. If the husband refuses to obtain therapeutic intervention and extricate the abu-sive behavior, the wife should not return to an abusive marriage. There should be a zero tolerance for abuse in the marriage.

Abusing a person violates Biblical principles. In Genesis 1:26-28 Moses records that human beings have been designed in the image of God. Because of that fact, we need to value fellow humans – particularly our spouses. Abuse of a human being is morally offensive and legally wrong. Abuse also violates what we commonly refer to as the 'Golden Rule' deliv-ered to us by Christ Himself:

> *"So, whatever you wish*
> *that others would do to you,*
> *do also to them, for this is the*
> *Law and the Prophets."*
> *[Matthew 7:12 – ESV]*

No one wants to be abused themselves, unless they are experiencing some type of serious mental health disorder. When a person engages in abusing their spouse, they are actually abusing their Creator as well.

The National Domestic Violence hotline indicates that 15% of women have experienced physical violence. Four percent of men have experienced physical violence. We see here that physical abuse can be perpetrated by either the husband or the wife. An average of twenty-four people per minute are victims of physical violence and many of these incidents are in the context of marriage. Forty percent of women and thirty-two percent of men surveyed indicated that they have experienced emotional abuse. These statistics are staggering and could be considered epidemic.

"A perfect marriage is just two imperfect people who refuse to give up on each other." [unknown]

I would challenge each husband and their wives to treat each other as 'segullah' which is a Hebrew concept that means "Treasured Possession". Moses uses this term in Exodus:

"Now therefore, if you will indeed obey My voice and keep My covenant, you shall be My 'treasured possession' among all peoples..."
[Exodus 19:5 – ESV]

Abandonment is the third reason, offered in rabbinical application of Original Testament, for divorce. Approximately eighteen years ago I worked with a couple in regards to marital counseling. Their hypothetical names are Bill and Brenda. Bill was a tall, athletic, and handsome guy. He had invested a considerable amount of time studying the scriptures.

He was adept at readily quoting Bible verses and was proficient in sharing his faith. Bill was confident and articulate. I didn't know much about Bill's family of origin and he just 'showed up' in our area. Bill was suave and a smooth-talking man. He claimed to have a deep and abiding relationship with the LORD. However, his words were not matched by his behavior.

Brenda was an attractive lady in her late twenties. She presented herself well physically and was a very kind and gentle person. Brenda was experiencing self-induced pressure to get married and begin a family because she was nearly thirty years of age. Brenda had several failed relationships prior to meeting Bill. She was also insecure and somewhat naïve. Brenda came from a good family of origin. Her father provided well for the family but was somewhat controlling. Brenda's mother was a soft-spoken, gentle, and loving mom.

Bill and Brenda met at a church gathering. Brenda was immediately attracted to Bill and they began dating. Looking back, it's quite apparent that Bill targeted Brenda as easy 'prey'. He quickly managed to put their relationship on fast-forward. The couple became sexually active at a very early stage in their association. They chose to become passionately involved prior to developing a healthy intimacy level and then enter the Covenant of Marriage. An unplanned pregnancy resulted, and turmoil became the operational word for their relationship.

Bill was addicted to drugs. He would have brief periods of time where he would experience sobriety and was able to hold a job effectively. Then he would just be gone.

Multiple times Brenda had no idea where he was or exactly what he was doing, and she feared the worst. When Bill would return, he would use his excellent communication skills and persuasive powers to convince Brenda that he was doing alright and had things under control.

Bill proved to be the master manipulator.

When Brenda's parents were informed of the unplanned pregnancy, they were shocked and disappointed. Brenda's father was absolutely enraged with Bill. His anger reached such a high level that he offered Brenda a considerable amount of money to abort the baby and discontinue her relationship with Bill. Brenda was adamantly pro-life and refused to comply with the bribe that her father offered. As you can imagine, the tension level between Brenda and her father reached a feverish pitch.

Brenda decided to accept the proposal offered by Bill and they were married. Her desire was to be a good wife and outstanding mother. I believe she thought that if she and Bill would marry then he would change his addictive behavior. She and Bill were married much to the chagrin of her father particularly. She gave birth to a beautiful baby girl. Brenda had the benefit of being the beneficiary of excellent maternal nurturing and was able to meet the needs of her child and became a very good mother. Bill continued his drug abuse and became an absentee father. He portrayed himself as a loving father and demonstrated that intermittently in the first few months after their child was delivered. Bill rapidly deteriorated in his ability to deal effectively with his addiction. He refused to become involved in rehabilitation efforts. He would be gone a weekend, a week, a month and then completely abandoned his wife and child. Brenda had no contact with him for two years. Bill provided no monetary support for his child. He completely 'ghosted' his family and his responsibilities as a husband and father.

Brenda rightly filed for divorce on the grounds of abandonment. The judge granted her petition for divorce and the marriage was nullified. Eighteen years passed and Bill was still in absentia. He never made any attempt to contact Brenda or check on the welfare of his child. Rabbinic scholars would heartily agree that Brenda had solid grounds to divorce Bill because of abandonment. Human beings are fashioned by their Creator for companionship. The plan of God for humans is to experience the ultimate level of companionship within the Covenant of Marriage.

Abandonment by a spouse breaks the bond of companionship that was intended by YHWH. The spouse that has experienced abandonment has obviously experienced abuse.

On a side note, I had the opportunity to individually work with Brenda's father who had wanted her to terminate her pregnancy. I challenged him about the fact that GOD hates the shedding of innocent blood and that is exactly what abortion would have accomplished. I encouraged him that the day his granddaughter was born he would have a complete change of heart. He didn't believe those words at the time. When he held that little blessing from GOD for the first time, he instantly became a loving grandfather. It's been amazing to watch the transformation that God has brought about in his life. Brenda and her father were able to reconcile. Brenda has since remarried and is doing well. Pray for Bill as we still have no idea where he is or if he is even alive. Brenda filed legal motions for the court to remove all parental rights from Bill. The judge ruled favorably on that petition and Bill, because of abandonment, had his parental rights revoked. Bill experienced the sowing and reaping principle as spoken by the prophet Hosea in the 8th century B.C.:

"For they sow the wind
and reap the whirlwind."
[Hosea 8:7 – ESV]

The ancient Romans used to cut open a pig and study the entrails
to determine the luckiest time to marry.
[Credit: 'the knot' website]
They also used this technique to
determine when to go to war. In
spite of this, the Roman Empire
lasted 500 years!!!

67

Adultery is specifically written as a cause for divorce. Abuse is attacking a human being who bears the image of God. Abandonment speaks against the first diagnosis in human history: "It is not good that man should be alone…" [Genesis 2:18 -ESV]. The original intent of YHWH is that a man and woman would enter the Covenant of Marriage and remain married. God specifically states in Malachi 2:16 that HE 'hates' divorce. HE hates divorce, but HE does not hate the divorcee. By working in the field of counseling for over forty, I have seen the devastating consequences of divorce and I can understand why God hates divorce.

Divorce impacts a wide array of individuals, not just the couple involved. Divorce is always rough on children regardless of their age. We as human beings are simply not perfect, and we all make mistakes and some of those mistakes are more consequential than others. Even when divorce occurs, God stands ready to forgive and reconcile humans to Himself.

YHWH chose His people Israel and demonstrated in numerous ways that HE valued them. We must prove to our spouse that we value them above all other human relationships.

We need to place the needs of our spouse ahead of our own personal desires. We must treasure our spouse and protect them. Paul wrote to the church at Corinth:

"…love always protects"
[I Corinthians 13:7 - ESV]

The Greek word for 'protects' is 'stege' and this literally means 'to cover' or 'to roof over' something. The idea of protecting something is inherent in this word. For example, we construct a roof over the garage to protect our cars. In the Jewish culture weddings are conducted with the couple standing under a 'chuppah' or covering. This canopy-like structure represents the home that the couple intends to build together. It symbolizes the need for the couple to protect each other. The chuppah may have been in Paul's thoughts when he penned the words above. We need to protect our spouses and our marriage. Agape love that is actualized will result in the husband and wife being completely committed to the other's well-being and protecting their marriage.

2400 years ago Nehemiah wrote these challenging words for us to study and apply:

> "...Remember the LORD,
> WHO is great and awesome,
> and fight for your brothers,
> your sons, your daughters,
> your wives and your homes."
> [Nehemiah 3:13]

In my counseling practice I always encourage couples to fight for their marriage. I challenge them to diligently pray about what YHWH would have them do, asking for wisdom and discernment in accordance with counsel included in the Book of James:

> "If any of you lacks wisdom,
> let him ask GOD, WHO gives
> generously to all without
> reproach, and it will be given
> him. But let him ask in faith,
> [James 1:5, 6 ESV]

Many marriages are terminated by divorce because the couple has just reached the point to where they give up. Keeping a marriage together and restoring the covenant is paramount in the program of YHWH. We need to value marriage and do everything in our power, inviting Divine intervention, to save and heal our marriages.

My theory is that the Biblical term for "Leave" that YHWH inspired Moses to write nearly 3,500 years ago is complemented by the terms Commitment and Agape. This is foundational for a healthy marriage covenant. It is the essential foundational bedrock that is enhanced by Intimacy and celebrated by Passion.

Moses was nearing the end of his earthly existence when GOD inspired him to write the Book of Deuteronomy which is comprised of three sermons. These three sermons focus on the faithfulness of YHWH to His covenant people – Israel. Moses spoke of HIS faithfulness to Israel in the past, the present and the future. He wrote these terrific words of encouragement:

> *"Be strong and courageous.*
> *Do not fear or be in dread of*
> *them, for it is the LORD*
> *your God Who goes with you.*
> *He will not leave you or forsake you."*
> *[Deuteronomy 31:6 – ESV]*

YHWH had entered a covenant relationship with Israel through Abraham in Genesis 12. Six hundred years later He was still proving His commitment to that covenant through Moses. YHWH continued to be true to that covenant when He Himself came to planet earth in order to redeem mankind. YHWH took on the veil of humanity and was beheld by His disciples. Jesus, YHWH incarnate makes the same covenant promise to those who follow Him:

> *"Go therefore and make disciples*
> *of all nations, baptizing them in*
> *the name of the Father, and of the*
> *Son, and of the Holy Spirit, teaching*
> *Them to observe all that I have*

Commanded you. And behold, I am
with you always, to the end of the age."
[Matthew 28:19,20 – ESV]

"..."I will never leave you nor
forsake you."
[Hebrews 13:5]

YESHUA bin YHWH, Jesus the Son of God, is the ultimate example of honoring the covenant of God. He laid down His life for His bride – the church. If both spouses adopt this type of unwavering commitment to the covenant of marriage then marriages will withstand the test of time.

Engagement rings and wedding
rings are placed on the 4th finger
of the left hand. It was thought
that there was a vein in that finger
that led directly to the heart.
[Credit: 'the knot' website]

None of us are perfect. We all make mistakes. We all sin and disobey God. Divorce happens sometimes for appropriate and inappropriate reasons. Regardless, God loves the person who divorces equally as much as the person who is fortunate enough to have never divorced. GOD is in the business of reconciling people to Himself. His ability and willingness to forgive is accentuated by Paul in the portion of his letter to believers in Colossae.

"And you, who were dead
in your trespasses and the
uncircumcision of your

*flesh, GOD made alive
together with HIM, having
forgiven us ALL our
trespasses, by canceling
the record of debt that
stood against us with its
legal demands. This He
set aside, nailing it to
the cross."*
[Colossians 2:13,14 – ESV]

There is no sin so great that our compassionate Creator and Redeemer is not able and willing to forgive. Come to Christ in the situation your find yourself in and call upon His Name. You will find forgiveness and compassion.

*"Everyone who calls on
the name of the LORD
will be saved".*
[Romans 10:13 – ESV]

Larry & Deanna Bell - 12/30/1972

Katye & Haskell Bell - 02/01/1946

Deanna & Larry Bell [Married 12/30/1972]

Jim and Nina Cleavenger - Married 03/01/1948

Kenan & Bethany Bell – Married 05/05/2012

Jessica Bell Page & Lloyd Page – Married 05/26/2021

Kenan Bell, Deanna Bell, Larry Bell & Jessica Bell

Bethany, Westray, Ivory Jane, Hudson & Kenan Bell

Violet & Sophia Gordon, Jessica Bell Page

Westray, Violet, Hudson, Ivory Jane & Sophia -Grands

CLEAVE – INTIMACY – PHILEO

M oses recorded in Genesis chapter two that there are three components to the covenant of marriage: leaving, cleaving, and
becoming "one flesh". I reviewed the concept of leaving and connected
that concept to commitment and agape love. It is time to transition into
a study of the second component of the covenant which is 'cleaving'. The
Hebrew word for cleave is 'dagaq'. James Strong interprets this Hebrew
word into English meaning: 'to hold fast to'; 'to cling to'; to be 'joined fast';
or to be 'glued to'. Moses uses the terminology of becoming 'one flesh' to
describe the sexual union which is the ultimate physical connection.

The New International Version translation of the scripture uses the word
"united" for cleave.

It is apparent to me that the intention behind the concept of cleaving to
one's spouse is an emotional and psychological connection. Cleaving consists of a variety of components.

Cleaving will be described in concert with "Intimacy" and "Phileo" love.

Cleaving relates to intimacy in marriage. This intimacy is the emotional bonding and connectedness that enables the marriage to grow
and be stable. When a couple comes to see me for marital counseling, I

briefly describe the three primary components of the marriage covenant recorded by Moses:

Leave – Commitment – Agape

Cleave – Intimacy – Phileo

One Flesh – Passion – Eros

I then will ask the husband this question: "Seeing that I have separated "Intimacy" and "Passion" – what is the first word that comes to your mind when I say the word "Intimacy"? At least ninety percent of the husbands have a one-word response: "Sex"! I almost always detect an expressive 'eye roll' from their spouse when hearing that response.

Sex is very important in the marriage covenant, but I indicate that we will discuss the sexual part of the relationship with the terminology of 'one flesh', 'passion', and 'eros' love.

On June 18, 1979, the time came for my bride to deliver our first-born child, Jessica Lauren Bell. We had prepared for that day by participating in childbirth classes. Thankfully, I was able to witness a 'normal' delivery. I hesitate to use the word normal as it appeared to be stressful to my bride and my daughter. The medical personnel cleaned Jessica up very quickly and checked her breathing. As quickly as possible, they brought Jessica to her mother and me. It was incredible to witness the miracle of birth. We both verbally affirmed our love for Jessica. We also physically affirmed our love for her by holding, embracing, and kissing her. Verbal and physical affirmation are essential in the bonding process. This was all an essential part of the bonding process. The bonding process conveys two very important principles to the newborn child. Those two principles are Significance and Security. We began conveying this special message to Jessica from the moment of birth that she was Significant to us and Secure with us. When I think back to the nine months prior to her birth, we also conveyed those messages to her.

"A good marriage is a
contest of generosity."
[Dianne Sawyer]

The ovum is the largest cell in the human body. The sperm is the smallest cell in the human body. It is somewhat humbling to come to the realization how very little I contributed to the miracle of conception!!! I attended an "ICTHUS Conference" in Wilmore, Ky in the 1970s. Dr. Donald Joy, a professor at Asbury Theological Seminary, mentioned in his seminar the goal of the sperm. The sperm 'swim fast, love hard, and die young". That's a great way to live your life if you're a sperm, but not a good idea if you are a young man who is not married! At the moment of ejaculation 40,000,000 sperm are released and one will win the race to penetrate the ovum. Life begins at that moment of conception. That large ovum realized its nascent fulfillment and became our daughter. Our daughter is unique and could have been one of the forty million – but she is that one. We strove to convey love to Jessica by making her know she was significant and secure. We desired to convince Jessica the profound truth contained in these words written by King David 3,000 years ago:

"For You formed my inward parts;
You knitted me together in my
mother's womb.
I praise You, for I am fearfully
and wonderfully made.
Wonderful are Your works;
my soul knows it very well."
[Psalm 139:13,14 – ESV]

During the dating time the man and woman are pursuing each other. They are attempting to win each other's attention, affection and eventual commitment. The relationship develops by proving to one another that they are significant and secure. If something is significant to us we value it. If something is significant to us, we place it in a position of importance. The cleaving aspect of the covenant of marriage is the emotional and psychological bonding necessary to unite the couple or 'glue them together'. Moses used the term 'one flesh' to refer to the sexual part of the covenant of marriage. The cleaving component could be referred to as being of 'one mind'. One-mindedness focused on meeting each other's emotional and psychological needs for significance and security.

Many people choose to become involved passionately [sexually] prior to entering the covenant of marriage. If a relationship is formed primarily with a sexual emphasis, it will quite likely not endure. A couple can be physically attracted to each other and engage sexually without proving they are significant and secure to one another. Some folks choose to enter a marriage and the primary component of their relationship is sexual in nature. They have not invested time in the emotional and psychological bonding necessary to meet the significance and security needs of one another. Many people, particularly men, mistake sex for intimacy.

This becomes problematic over time and that couple would have a high likelihood of divorcing if the passionate part of the relationship is accentuated to the exclusion, or minimization, of the cleaving or intimacy component.

What is necessary for a couple to cleave and become intimately connected? Obviously, there are multiple components to consider in how to cleave to your spouse. There are very practical considerations that we can choose to develop and make an operational reality in our marriages. The first to be considered is the area of communication. The great majority of couples

*who come for marital counseling agree that they experience serious diffi-
culties in the area of communication.*

*Communication is a two-way street. Communication involves a sender
and receiver.*

*True communication includes reciprocity and involvement of both parties.
This is not a chauvinist statement – most women talk more than men. You
can show me exceptions to this but 90% of the couples I have worked with
agree that is accurate. True communication cannot be one person doing
all the 'sending' and one person doing all the 'receiving'. An exchange is
critical. A willingness to speak and a willingness to truly listen are absolutely essential for real communication to be achieved.*

Put down the cell phone!!!

*The 'Red Green Show' enjoyed fifteen successful seasons on television
from 1991-2006. Red would assemble his buddies for "Men's Anonymous"
meetings in the Possum Lodge. The men would simultaneously recite their
Men's Prayer:*

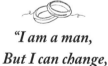

*"I am a man,
But I can change,
If I have to,
I guess"*

*The majority of husbands whom I have worked with need to increase the
number of words they share with their wives. Sometimes wives must
consolidate their words so there is time for an actual exchange. Many*

wives have shared with me that they keep talking in hope that their hus-band will eventually respond. This is quite frustrating to wives in gen-eral. Both the husband and the wife need to be sending communication and receiving communication.

Men tend to be reluctant and reticent in sharing their feelings.

"Fools" said I, "You do not know
Silence like a cancer grows
Hear my words that I might
teach you
Take my arms that I might
reach you
But my words like silent raindrops fell
And echoed in the wells of silence
[The Sound of Silence
Simon & Garfunkel – 1964]

Our culture generally pressures men to not reveal their true feelings. In fact, men are often taught to suppress their feelings rather than express them. We are programmed by our Creator with a variety of emotions. These emotions are designed to be expressed appropriately. If we inter-nalize our emotions, we are creating undue stress for ourselves that will negate a positive communication exchange with our spouse.

The state of Wyoming has the highest marriage rate in the United States. The state of Arkansas has the lowest divorce rate.
[United State Census]

Communication in a marriage needs concern more than just superficial topics. Couples need to be discussing finances and budgeting. Couples need to be discussing parenting and discipline issues if children are still at home. Couples should be involved in talking about mutual hopes and dreams. Practical issues of where the family will spend Thanksgiving, Christmas, and other major holidays require mutual input and sharing of expectations. Planning for the future events is critical like what to do in the event of a catastrophic medical event. Do you want to be on life supports for extended periods of time?

What type of funeral arrangements would you prefer?

In my opinion, couples should be able to discuss anything. It is vital that the husband and wife be the very best of friends. They should be able to confide in one another with absolute trust. My wife and I have been married for 48 years. Deanna is my best friend. I do not believe that there is anything we cannot discuss at this point in our marriage. I will not portray that we agree about everything because that is not true. However, we respect each other and mutually invest effort to communicate. I have some crazy ideas on occasion. If I want to get an honest opinion about my idea I will share that with my wife. I might even preface this by: "Hey Dee, I have a crazy idea I want to run by you. I don't want my brothers or your brothers or our kids to know about this!" I can trust her completely with my idea and am positive it will remain confidential.

Every married couple will experience turmoil in their marriage at some point. Try to point out a couple in the scriptures that was free from turmoil. When you study the life of Abraham, he brought significant stress into his marriage with Sarah and Sarah assisted.

Sarah was aging and her perspective appeared to be that her 'biological clock' had stopped concerning her ability to conceive and give birth. She was aware that GOD had promised Abraham that he would be the father of multitudes. That promise could only be fulfilled if Abraham had a son to perpetuate his lineage. Perhaps she perceived that GOD needed some help since she was in her late eighties and barren. She approached Abraham with a plan to assist GOD with HIS promise. She thought it would be a good idea for Abraham to marry her Egyptian handmaiden, Hagar, and have the son of promise through her. I wonder if Abraham took a step back, stroked his beard, contemplated, and replied: "Sarah, of all the ideas you've ever had, certainly this is one of the best!!" Abraham did marry Hagar, which was socially acceptable in the culture at that time, and Hagar gave birth to a son. The son was named Ishmael. He was a 'wild donkey' of a man and brought a considerable amount of turmoil into the lives of Sarah and Abraham. However, GOD is always true to HIS promises and when Abraham was 100 years old, and Sarah was 90 years old she gave birth to a son. That son was named Isaac and the Abrahamic lineage was secure and would continue for 2,000 years when the MESSIAH would be born. Abraham, the first to be designated a Hebrew, experienced marital discord. Ishmael and his descendants became the Arabic nations who are now mostly Islamic. The Islamic nations believe that the lineage of promise by GOD is through Ishmael.

Therefore, we can see that the animosity between the lineage of Isaac and Ishmael persists today, originated with the plot developed 4,000 years ago by Abraham and Sarah. I wonder how many discussions Abraham and Sarah had about the stressful impact of their mutual agreement to involve Hagar?

Isaac, the son of promise, would eventually marry Rebekah. Rebekah had difficulty in conceiving for years but eventually GOD enabled her to become pregnant with twins. The pregnancy was not progressing exactly as she imagined. It was a tumultuous pregnancy and she finally prayed to GOD to determine what was transpiring. The answer given by GOD is described by Moses:

*"Two nations are in your womb, and two peoples from within you
shall be divided; the one shall be stronger than the other,
the older shall serve the younger."*
[Genesis 25:23 – ESV]

*After Isaac and Rebekah completed their childbirth classes, Rebekah gave
birth to her twin sons. The first of the boys to enter the delivery room
was a hairy little guy with a reddish complexion and they named him
Esau. The name Esau means 'Red'. As Esau was entering the world, his
younger brother was holding onto the heel of Esau. The second boy was
named Jacob and his name means trickster, supplanter or tripper-upper.
The prophecy that Rebekah received from God became true as Esau for-
feited his birthright and Jacob would be the son whom God would work
through to continue the Messianic lineage.*

*Jacob's name would later be changed to Israel. Israel became the father of
sons who would become the progenitors of the twelve tribes of Israel. If
you want to discover how YHWH can work through dysfunction, study
the marriages of Jacob. The woman Jacob loved and desired to marry
was the daughter of his uncle, Laban. Her name was Rachel, and she is
described as being beautiful in 'form and appearance' [Genesis 29:17 –
ESV]. Laban made a deal with Jacob that if he worked for seven years,
he could have Rachel as his wife. After the seven years were completed a
honeymoon tent was prepared. In the darkness of the night Laban sent his
eldest daughter, Leah, into the tent for the marriage to be consummated.
Laban justified his actions by informing Jacob that it was their custom
to have the eldest daughter marry first.*

*Laban then offered Jacob another deal that would cause him to have to
work an additional seven years to be able to have his beloved Rachel as
his wife. Jacob loved Rachel so much he agreed to this extraordinary plan.
You can imagine the jealousy and rivalry that would evolve between
Leah and Rachel. In fact, the scripture records: "When the LORD saw*

that Leah was hated, he opened her womb." [Genesis 29:31 -ESV]. Hated by whom? Perhaps Jacob was not too thrilled at the switch that Uncle Laban had orchestrated, and he took it out on Leah. Quite likely Rachel had developed hatred for her older sister who delayed her wedding plans. Jacob and Rachel both had to have been disappointed at Laban for his actions They both likely demonstrated displaced anger toward Leah.

Leah was able to conceive, and she gave birth to a son named Reuben. Rachel was barren. Leah gave birth to a second son named Simeon and Rachel remained barren. Leah delivered a third son named Levi and she thought that the birth of this third son would grant her favor in the sight of Jacob. After delivering her fourth consecutive son, Judah, Leah would discontinue bearing children. So now Jacob has four sons with a woman he had not intended to marry and no sons with the woman, Rachel, whom he intended to marry. This family was experiencing high levels of conflict.

Rachel was desperate and concerned that she would lose the love of her husband because of her barrenness. She convinced Jacob to marry her servant, Bilhah, and have a child with her. Jacob agreed and Bilhah gave birth to a son named Dan.

[Echoes of Abraham, Sarah and Hagar!!!]. Bilhah conceived and presented Jacob with another son named Naphtali. Now that Rachel is presenting Jacob with sons via a surrogate, Leah becomes jealous because now she perceives Rachel is winning the battle for the affection of Jacob.

Leah presented Jacob with her servant, Zilpah. Jacob married Zilphah and she gave birth to Gad and subsequently another son named Asher. Conflict abounded in the family of Jacob. It even intensifies more as Jacob and Leah come together once again and Issachar is born. Leah would be enabled to give birth one more time to a son named Zebulun.

In order to attempt to keep things straight, let's look at the 'score'. Jacob and Leah have six sons together. Jacob and Bilhah had two sons together. Jacob and Zilpah had two sons together. Jacob and these three women have produced a total of ten sons. Rachel must have been a psychological basket case. She would finally be blessed by YHWH and HE enabled her to conceive. She would give birth to a very famous son named Joseph. Rachel would conceive again years later. As she completed giving birth to her second son, Benjamin, she would die. Rachel was buried on the way to Ephrathah, which is Bethlehem. There is a tomb there to this day. Women of Israel go to the tomb of Rachel and pray for their barren family members and friends. I had the opportunity to visit the tomb of Rachel in 1985.

The final family configuration for the house of Jacob, whose sons would be raised up to lead the twelve tribes of Israel:

- ➢ *Jacob and Leah had six sons*
  - ○ *Reuben*
  - ○ *Simeon*
  - ○ *Levi*
  - ○ *Judah*
  - ○ *Issachar*
  - ○ *Zebulun*
- ➢ *Jacob and Bilhah had two sons*
  - ○ *Dan*
  - ○ *Naphtali*
- ➢ *Jacob and Zilpah had two sons*
  - ○ *Gad*
  - ○ *Asher*
- ➢ *Jacob and Rachel had two sons*
  - ○ *Joseph*
  - ○ *Benjamin*

Talk about a family that was a hotbed for stress and conflict!! This could be a primetime television drama. The family of Jacob demonstrated an incredibly high level of dysfunctionality. Despite this, YHWH worked through this dysfunction and established the nation of Israel which would be organized under twelve tribes. The sons of Jacob became those tribal leaders. If you think that God cannot use you because of the baggage of your family of origin – think again!! Every marriage has stress...no marriage is perfect.

*The costliest divorce, in terms of
money, probably goes to Microsoft
entrepreneur, Bill Gates. He and his
ex-wife, Melinda, split $146,000,000,000.
That's billion...with a 'B'
Jeff Bezos, of Amazon fame, divorced
his wife - Mackenzie. She 'settled' for
$36,000,000,000!!!
She'll get by with
a little help from her friends!!!*

CONFLICT RESOLUTION

We are not informed of the details about how Jacob and his family resolved their conflicts. Conflicts occur in every marriage. How do you resolve conflicts? What follows is a discussion on conflict resolution. I often have clients participate in a conflict resolution exercise with that is entitled: 'Resolve to Resolve'. When I opened my first private counseling practice in Bridgeport, WV, I asked my wife for a suggestion on what to name my practice. She came up with an excellent recommendation – "Resolutions,

Inc."Here is an overview of the exercise which is based upon the acronym:
'RESOLVED'.

RESOLVE TO RESOLVE – *Conflict Resolution Exercise*

- ➢ *R – Remember to attack the problem, not the person*

- ➢ *E – Escaping the problem does not solve it*

- ➢ *S – Speak the truth in love*

- ➢ *O – Out of control is out of line*

- ➢ *L – Listen so you can resolve, not so you can win*

- ➢ *V – Veto generalizations, boil down to specific issues*

- ➢ *E – Explore your options for reaching both of your goals*

- ➢ *D – Discipline yourself to stay on the topic*

Remember to attack the problem, not the person

Remember to attack the person, not the problem. We all develop habitual
methods of dealing with conflict. When some people perceive conflict,
they immediately become aggressive and usually have the perspective
that, "I'm going to win this!!" That type of perspective is followed with an
aggressive exchange and verbal volley. The aggressive person often tends
to talk faster, louder, and demonstrate intimidating posturing.

One lady shared with me that her husband, who was much taller, would 'hover' over her whether seated or standing. He would position himself in such a way to emphasize he was looking down upon her. I personally witnessed him becoming irate in a counseling session and he literally stood up and 'hovered' over his wife. He meandered around my desk and attempted his intimidation over me. As you can imagine that session did not end well. He chose to storm out of the office. This was imposing to her and elicited a 'fight or flight'

response, and she consistently chose flight, or disengagement. They might even have in mind, consciously or subconsciously, that they will impose their will if necessary. Overly aggressive people can become so consumed with winning that they will engage in hurtful, and potentially damaging verbal exchanges. They know where the other person is the most vulnerable and can become willing to 'hit below the belt'. The use of profanity and name-calling frequently accompany an aggressive approach to conflict. These behaviors will never resolve the conflict effectively.

"Ad Hominem"
It occurs when someone
attacks directly the person
making an argument rather
than criticizing the argument
itself.
[fallacyinlogic.com]

Other folks just do not like to deal with conflict. They immediately become uncomfortable when tension surfaces in their relationship. They prefer non-engagement in hopes that the conflict will just dissipate. They will avoid actively engaging in the resolution of the conflict. Many times, they will just 'give in' – with hope that will end the conflict. That response

might end the tension for a brief period, but the conflict is not resolved. The person who is aggressive will have perceived that they 'won', or they were 'right' just because their spouse disengaged. The conflict, that was not resolved, does not disappear. The person who 'gave in' will store that unresolved issue in an emotional 'backpack'. That unresolved conflict will quite likely resurface at some future point. The unresolved conflict becomes ammunition for a future blow-up. The emotional backpack only has so much capacity to contain turmoil. There will come a time when the person will, of necessity, need to unload the unresolved conflicts. It is far better to deal with conflict as it occurs, rather than storing multiple unresolved conflicts over time. If a person develops the habit of storing conflict, rather than resolving conflict, they are inviting physical and mental health concerns. Conflict that is not dealt with becomes internalized. Internalized conflict can be manifested by psychological and somatic symptoms. Anxiety and depression can be a direct result of unresolved conflict. The ability to concentrate can be impaired and energy levels are depleted. A person can lose self-esteem and confidence in their interactions with others outside of the family. Ulcers, irritable bowel syndrome, arrhythmia and significant headaches are a few examples of somatic reactions to internalized unresolved conflict.

Attacking the person instead of the problem will not prove to be beneficial. Attacking the person is an assault on their self-esteem. Attacking the person instead of the problem is disrespectful to a fellow image-bearer.

Husband: Steak?
Wife: NO
Husband: Chicken?
Wife: NO
Husband: Italian?
Wife: NO
Husband: Then what do you want?

Wife: It's up to you!!!

Escaping the problem does not solve it

The Apostle Paul wrote these words to the church at Ephesus in the first century:

> *"Be angry and do not sin,*
> *do not let the sun go down*
> *on your anger."*
> *[Ephesians 4:26,27]*

We can observe in these verses that anger is one of the multiple emotions that our Creator programmed human beings with the ability to express. The overriding scriptural principle in dealing with our emotions is that we should express our emotions appropriately, not let them control us to the point of sin. The emotion of anger will be discussed under the 'Out of Control is Out of Line' principle. It is apparent here that YHWH directs us to 'not let the sun go down on your anger'. When I ask couples to interpret what that means, the majority respond with a statement they likely heard from their mothers, "Don't go to bed mad"! That response is quite likely connected with these verses written to believers in Ephesus, which is located in western Turkey.

It is difficult to present 'guarantees' in conflict resolution, however, there are general guidelines that allow us to follow a course of wisdom. In general, the earlier that a conflict is addressed and tackled it is less complicated to resolve. I've had couples share with me the following scenario on a frequent basis. A conflict will arise in the early evening and the exchange becomes heated. Both spouses make a mental determination that they will not speak to each other. The silence becomes deafening as the tension mounts. Though nothing is being verbalized it is obvious to the children that their parents are quite upset with each other. The couple continues their passive-aggressive approach, and no verbal interaction occurs for several hours. The couple heads to bed and both stubbornly refuse to 'break the ice' as they retreat to their foxholes, which happen to be in the same bed. No talking, no expression of intimacy and certainly passion is absolutely not happening. Each of them has difficulty sleeping and the problem continues to occupy their thoughts. As morning approaches, plans for the day are reviewed. Time to awaken, get breakfast prepared, get the kids off to school and head to work. They have zero time to work on the conflict and they still are adamant to wait the other person out. This communication chess game now transfers to the work setting. The couple is distracted and not able to focus well to complete their job responsibilities and thankfully the workday ends. The couple heads home and they are tired from lack of sleep and frustrated from their work performance. When you're tired and frustrated, conflict resolution becomes more arduous.

It is more logical to engage in the resolution of the conflict as quickly as possible. A friend of mine who worked with me at the State Vocational Rehabilitation Office in West Virginia had a plaque on her wall that read: "When emotion enters, logic departs". Though not a Biblical saying, it contains a significant measure of truth. I've usually observed in marital counseling that one spouse wants to actively pursue the resolution of conflict and the other tends to want to withdraw, avoid, and escape. A higher percentage of husbands choose the path of escape in hopes that the conflict will just evaporate. What happens is that the conflict does not disappear, in fact it becomes ammunition for a future fight.

"Only two things are necessary to keep one's wife happy. One is to let her think she is having her own

way. The other is letting her have
her own way."
[Lyndon B. Johnson, #36]

Escaping the problem certainly does not result in resolution of the conflict;
it simply delays when resolution can be realized. If conflict is not resolved
habitually, then the relationship will eventually suffer notable damage.
Unresolved conflict turns into resentment and bitterness. Bitterness that
becomes embedded will wreak havoc in a marriage. The accumulation
of unresolved conflict drives a wedge between spouses and often ends
in divorce.

God Himself is in the reconciliation business as the song 'Hark the Herald
Angels" proclaims: "God and sinners reconciled". His challenge to us is to
be ambassadors who are peace brokers.

"If it is possible,
so far as it depends on you,
live peaceable with all."
[Romans 12:18 – ESV]

"Blessed are the peacemakers
for they shall be called
the sons of GOD."
[Matthew 5:8 - ESV]

It is preferable and more expedient to work on resolving conflict at the
earliest possible juncture. I challenge couples to pray about the conflict and
then ask themselves this question:

"What can I do to resolve this conflict?" If both parties activate this perspec-
tive, then the process of reconciling the issue can be more quickly achieved.

*Tom Harmon won the Heisman
Trophy at the University of
Michigan in 1940. He became
a bomber pilot for the U.S. Army.
In April 1943 Harman was shot
down during a dogfight with
Japanese Zeros. He parachuted
to safety and was the only survivor.
In August 1944, Harmon married
actress and model Elyse Knox.
Harmon had saved the silk parachute
that enabled his survival. Elyse used
the silk parachute as material for her
wedding dress.
[Wikipedia]
The Tom Harmons had three
children. My wife is a big fan of
Mark Harmon in his role as Leroy
Jethro Gibbs on NCIS!!*

Speak the truth in love

*The first word in this phrase is essential in achieving the resolution of
conflict. If we are not willing to talk about the issue, we diminish the
likelihood of resolution. I am personally aware of a couple who lived in
an extremely small house of approximately 1,000 square feet. They also
had three children living with them.*

Conflict arose and the couple literally went six months without speaking a word to each other.

The issue continued to fester unresolved for 180 days.

If we continue to disengage, we eventually eliminate the possibility of resolution. YHWH has given us as human beings the highest level of communication abilities of any of HIS creation. In fact, human beings are the only portion of GOD'S creation who knows that GOD exists and can choose to develop a personal relationship with HIM. We can use our high level of verbal communication to be positive, uplifting and encouraging to our spouse. Or we can unwisely choose to be derogatory, demeaning and abusive with our words.

Truth has a long shelf life with no expiration date. It is never obsolete, outdated, or archaic, or stale.
Steve Lawson

Think back to your high school days for a moment. I imagine that you can remember someone, a friend, teacher, or coach who said something that made a positive impact on you. It is also quite likely that you can retrieve from your memory bank the very words that someone said to you that were hurtful. My high school baseball coach approached me after practice one evening. He said: "Bell, you have deceptive speed – you are slower than you look!" I was 6' 1" tall and weighed 135 pounds at the time. I was very thin and lanky and was not blessed with great speed. He said those words to me over 50 years ago and I can clearly hear them today. As a result of that assessment, he always batted me last in the lineup, even

though I had a high on base percentage. When I progressed to play at the American Legion level my coach batted me in the lead-off position. He recognized my good on-base percentage.

He also realized that you didn't necessarily have to be fast to steal bases and score. If you could read the pitcher correctly, you could get the jump needed to steal the base. I never was thrown out stealing a base. I certainly do not hold this against my high school coach. I am simply sharing how powerful words can be. His words became embedded into my memory.

Perhaps no one knows the power of words more than the advertising industry. Forty-seven years ago, in 1974, the advertising department of the McDonalds Corporation developed a jingle to help us remember the ingredients of their Big Mac sandwich. For those of us old enough to remember, I bet you can sing that jingle right now and you have not heard it in over four decades. That jingle became an earworm:

> *"Two all-beef patties,*
> *special sauce, lettuce,*
> *cheese, pickles, onions,*
> *on a sesame-seed bun."*

An earworm refers to a song becoming 'stuck' in our minds. The chorus of a song that you keep reviewing in your mind involuntarily is an example of an earworm. This same concept translates into the how we use our words in conflict resolution. Words become part of our memory and are readily retrievable. Words have power that can be positive or negative. If you have a pistol, and you pull the trigger, the bullet discharges. The bullet will strike a target.

Once the bullet discharges you can't get it back. It's the same with our words. Once our words are spoken, they will produce an immediate positive or negative impact. Children who are repeatedly degraded verbally by their parents develop insecurities and self-esteem issues. The same principle is true in our marriages. If we use our words inappropriately, we can expect negative and potentially dire consequences.

"What counts in making a happy marriage is not so much how compatible you are, but how you deal with incompatibility."
[Leo Tolstoy]

I have worked with hundreds of couples in dealing with conflict resolution. I have never heard one wife say: "If my husband just cursed me out more things would be great."

Profanity has never proven to be an effective way of communication in a marriage. Profanity is demeaning and intimating. Directing profane words at our spouse does not lead to a constructive interaction. Paul wrote these challenging words concerning profanity nearly 2,000 years ago:

"Let your speech always be gracious, seasoned with salt, so that you may know how you ought to answer each person."
[Colossians 4:6 – ESV]

"But now you must put them all away: anger, wrath, malice, slander obscene talk from your

mouth.”
[Colossians 3:8 – ESV]

I studied for my Bachelor of Science Degree at Fairmont State College. The final two years of my college experience I lived in a fraternity house. My language morphed into typical fraternity vernacular. I could spew out profanity nearly as easily and frequently as breathing.

I found the "f-bomb" to be the most versatile word available. It could be positive or negative, verb or adverb, demeaning or even complimentary. In August of 1976 my life, and my language patterns, changed for the good. I became a disciple of YESHUA. I immediately discontinued the use of profanity. I won't say that was a class 'A' miracle like parting the Red Sea, but probably a class 'B' miracle. I am not going to portray to you that in the last 45 years I have never cursed. However, profanity is thankfully an extremely rare occurrence in my interaction with people.

The kind of words that we use in communicating with our spouse is of utmost importance. If we discontinue the use of profanity, we will discover it enhances the likelihood of a much more positive interaction. Three thousand years ago, Solomon provided words of wisdom concerning the kind of words that should be evident in our speech:

> *"Gracious words are like*
> *a honeycomb, sweetness*
> *to the soul and health to*
> *the body.”*
> *[Proverbs 16:24 – ESV]*

Being complimentary to our spouse is a positive way to bless them. Focus on their positive attributes. Provide verbal feedback that will enhance their self-esteem. Use your words to be an encouragement. King Solomon used his words to flatter his Shulamite bride.

"Behold, you are beautiful, my love,
behold you are beautiful! Your eyes
are doves behind your veil. Your hair
is like a flock of goats leaping down
slopes of Gilead.
Your teeth are like a flock of shorn
ewes that have come up from the
washing, all of which bear twins,
and not one among them has lost
its young.
Your lips are like a scarlet thread,
and your mouth is lovely.
Your cheeks are like halves of a
pomegranate behind your veil."
[Song of Solomon 4:1-3 – ESV]

These are compliments from King Solomon three thousand years ago. Not sure how your bride would receive the hair and teeth comparison today!! Probably a good idea to update and finetune your complimentary words!

I have never heard a husband say: "If she would just yell at me more and nag me more then things would be better." The kind of words we use are critical. Also, the volume with which we project our words is a key to pave the way to a more appropriate exchange. Often times yelling includes verbiage that becomes a personal attack. If someone is yelling at you, does that incline you to want to listen and communicate? I am not aware of anyone who genuinely appreciates being yelled at or scolded.

Being willing to talk is critical. There must be participation from both parties for actual communication to be occurring. It is also possible to say too much. Moderation is an ingredient that should be included in the communication mixture.

"When words are many,
transgression is not lacking,
but whoever restrains his
lips is prudent."
[Proverbs 10:19 – ESV]

It is imperative to speak the truth. The ninth command of the Ten Commandments states:

"You shall not bear false
witness against your
neighbor."
[Exodus 20:16- ESV]]

"…you shall not lie
to one another."
[Leviticus 19:11 – ESV]

Lying causes immediate hurt and harm in the marriage or in any relationship. Lying diminishes the ability to be trusted. Habitual lying eliminates the ability to be trusted. When trust is lost, the marriage relationship is in consequential trouble. Lying is a seed that when planted it germinates and takes on a life of its own. Lies beget lies. According to the BBC Website a lie possesses three essential features:

➢ *A lie communicates some information*

➢ *A liar intends to deceive or mislead*

➢ *The liar believes what they are saying is not true*

Lying is intentional deception. When my favorite daughter was in the 8th grade, she asked my permission to go to a sleep-over at

103

the house of a friend. She indicated that several girls would be in attendance. There was implicit pressure that if she was not able to attend, she would be a social outcast. I indicated that it sounded like a good time and then asked a simple question: "Will her parents be there?" My daughter replied: "Why wouldn't they be there?" I was immediately suspicious of that response. I informed her that I would discuss this with her mother, and we would let her know. I was friends with the father of the girl hosting the sleep-over, so I called him. I invited he and his wife over to play cards on the evening of the event and he declined indicating that they would be out of town the entire weekend. Obviously, my daughter was not allowed to participate in this unchaperoned party.

Did my daughter lie to me? In my opinion -yes!! She gave me some information, but not the whole truth. She knew that if she presented the entire picture, she would not be allowed to attend the sleep-over. She was being deliberately deceptive and that is lying.

> *"Lying lips are an abomination*
> *to the LORD, but those who act*
> *faithfully are HIS delight."*
> *{Proverbs 12:22 – ESV}*

There are people who believe that lying can be justified. People attempt to rationalize that lying is acceptable if it is done with 'good intention'. That seems to be an oxymoronic perspective to me. Lying is always wrong. It is always better to be truthful. Lies perpetuate more lies. It must be mentally exhausting to habitually lie. People who lie habitually tell lies that are lies.

> *"No man has a good enough*
> *memory to be a successful liar."*

[Abraham Lincoln]

I worked with a man whose wife had been committing adultery with the same man for seven years. It is almost unfathomable to me that she was able to be actively involved with another man for this amount of time undetected. It would be fascinating to be able to calculate the number of lies that she told her husband in those 2,555 days. She told hundreds, and perhaps thousands of lies to him. When her unfaithfulness was exposed, and her lies became evident the marriage was destroyed. The person who has been the recipient of lies experiences betrayal and disrespect.

The two busiest marriage days in
Las Vegas are New Year's Day
and Valentine's Day

The disciple John records the words of Christ in presenting the origin of lies and lying:

> *"You are of your father the devil,*
> *and your will is to do your father's*
> *desires. He was a murderer from*
> *the beginning and does not stand*
> *in the truth, because there is no*
> *truth in him. When he lies, he*
> *speaks out of his own character,*
> *for he is a liar and the father of lies"*
> *[John 8:44 – ESV]*

There is a spiritual battle being waged in this world. God is the author of truth and the devil is the 'father of lies'. When we lie, we choose evil and darkness. If we lie to our spouse we can expect to damage the relationship by diminishing trust. Trust is an integral part of the covenant of marriage. Absolute truth is being demonized in our society. There is a condescending notion that there is no 'Absolute Truth'. I believe that 'Absolute Truth' is found in the scriptures which are inspired by YHWH. Absolute truth teaches me that lying is always wrong. Lying is something that everyone must deal with appropriately. There is no human that lives their entire life without telling a lie. Abraham lied to Pharoah about Sarah being his wife. Peter lied and denied that he even knew the LORD. Lying is a common malady for all of humanity. When we lie, we must admit it, ask forgiveness for it and make restitution if necessary. We need to speak the truth in love to one another in the marriage covenant. Truth builds trust and trust nourishes the covenant of marriage. King David offers advice on having a life of integrity:

*"O LORD, who shall sojourn
in your tent? Who shall dwell
on your holy hill? He who
walks blamelessly and does
what is right and speaks the
truth in his heart."
[Psalm 15:1,2 – ESV]*

The Apostle Paul wrote these encouraging and challenging words to the believers in Ephesus nearly 2,000 years ago:

*"...speaking the truth in love,
we are to grow up in every way
into him who is the head, into
Christ."
[Ephesians 4:15 – ESV]*

Speak the truth in love to your spouse. Speaking the truth is simply being honest and transparent. Lies have a way of becoming known. If we are truthful, we are living a life of integrity and inviting the blessing of YHWH in our live and marriages. Two thousand years ago, James wrote these challenging words to believers:

"So the tongue is a small member, yet it boasts of great things. How great a forest is set ablaze by such a small fire, a world of unrighteousness. The tongue is set among our members, staining the whole body, setting on fire the entire course of life, and set on fire by hell. For every kind of beast and bird, of reptile and sea creature, can be tamed and has been tamed by mankind, but no human being can tame the tongue. It is a restless evil, full of deadly poison. With it we bless our LORD And FATHER, and with it we curse people who are made in the likeness of GOD. From the same mouth come blessing and cursing. My brothers, these things ought not to be so."
[James 3:5-10 – ESV]

Our LORD admonished HIS disciples saying: "I tell you, on the day of judgment people will give account for every careless word they speak, for by your words you will be justified, and by your words you will be condemned *[Matthew 12:36,37 -ESV]. Speak the truth in love to your spouse.*

Expensive Celebrity Wedding Dresses
Serena Williams - $3,500,000
Victoria Swarovski - $1,000,000
Kim Kardashian - $500,000
Salma Hayek - $434,000
Kate Middleton - $454,000
Khiara Ferragni - $420,000
Coleen Rooney - $392,000
Amal Clooney - $380,000
Mariah Carey - $250,000
Marie-Chantal Miller - $225,000
Elizabeth Tayor - $187,931
Catherine Zeta-Jones - $140,000
Princess Diana - $115,000
Jessica Biel - $100,000
Victoria Beckham - $100,000
Melania Trump - $100,000
Madonna - $80,000
Nicky Hilton- $77,000
Grace Kelly - $60,000
[By Blair Donovan and
Tess Petak...Brides.com
12/18/2020]

5 Deadly Terms Used By A Woman

"Fine" – This is a word women use to end an argument when she knows she is right and you need to stop talking.

"Nothing" – means something and you you should be worried.

"Go ahead" – do not confuse this with permission. It's a dare and don't even think about it!

"Whatever" – a woman's way of calling you an idiot.

"That's ok" – she is thinking long and hard on how and when you will pay for your mistakes.

Bonus Word:
"Wow!" – This is not a compliment. She is amazed that one person could be so clueless!!!
[Just_4Jokes / Instagram]

Out of control is out of line

The fourth principle in the 'RESOLVED' acronym is designed to study anger and how to express anger appropriately. We are programmed by our Creator with the powerful emotion of anger. The scripture does not say: "Don't be angry". The scripture does say: "Be angry and do not sin" [Ephesians 4:26 – ESV]. The issue becomes how do we express our anger and not sin? There are several characteristics of a 'fool' described in the Book of Proverbs. One of those characteristics describes the person who is controlled by his anger.

> *"A fool gives full vent to his anger, but a wise man holds it in check."*
> *[Proverbs 29:11 – Holman Christian Standard Bible]*

King David had many times in his life where he became angry. He wrote about those times in several Psalms.

> *"Refrain from anger, and forsake wrath! Fret not yourself, it tends only to evil."*
> *[Psalm 37:8 – ESV]*

The Hebrew word for anger is 'aph' which can literally mean 'flared nostrils'. You've probably seen the cartoons where the matador is taunting the bull with his red cape attempting to provoke the bull into charging.

This infuriates the bull, and the cartoonist depicts the raging bull then charging the matador with its nostrils flaring. This demonstrates the frightening power of anger.

There are multiple examples in the scriptures of people being enraged. Cain and Abel [Genesis 4] had presented offerings to God. God was pleased with the offering of Abel. GOD had 'no regard' for the offering of Cain. This resulted in Cain becoming 'very angry, and his face fell'. God confronted Cain and gave him the opportunity to do what was right and his offering would be accepted. God had told Cain: "...sin is crouching at the door. Its desire is contrary to you, but you must rule over it." Sin is depicted as an animal crouching and ready to pounce. Peter tells us who this crouching animal is:

"Be sober-minded,
be watchful. Your
adversary the devil
prowls around like a
roaring lion, seeking
someone to devour.
Resist him, firm in
your faith..."
[I Peter 5:7,8 – ESV]

Cain did not resist, and he did not stand firmly in faith. The uncontrolled anger of Cain culminated with the first murder in human history as he slew his brother Abel in the field. Uncontrolled anger can lead to the most devastating consequences imaginable.

Moses had entered the "SHEKINAH" cloud of glory at Mt Sinai to interact with YHWH. Moses spent forty days receiving information from God concerning the Law Code and the Sacrificial System. As he

111

descended Mt. Sinai and approached the Israelite encampment, he heard the sound of singing.

> *"And as soon as he came near*
> *the camp and saw the calf and*
> *the dancing, Moses' anger*
> *burned hot, and he threw the*
> *tablets out of his hands and broke*
> *them at the foot of the mountain."*
> *[Exodus 32:19 – ESV]*

The Israelites had grown impatient while Moses was with GOD. They crafted a golden calf idol, which was Apis, the 'bull god' of Egypt. The Israelites were engaged in a pagan worship service and this caused Moses to become red hot with anger. He became so angry that he broke the original copy of the Ten Commandments written by the finger of God. This lead GOD to provide a second set of tablets and these were quite likely the first Xerox copy in the history of humanity!

King David lusted after Bathsheba. He committed adultery and Bathsheba became pregnant. King David became involved in pre-meditated murder as he devised a plot to have her husband, Uriah the Hittite, killed on the battlefield. He executed Uriah in order to cover his sin and allow himself to marry Bathsheba. He was confronted by the prophet, Nathan, who told him a parabolic story of a rich man who had stolen the only lamb of a poor man to offer to his dinner guests. Nathan asked David what should happen to that man.

> *"Then David's anger was greatly*
> *kindled against the man, and he*
> *said to Nathan, "As the LORD*
> *lives, the man who has done this*
> *deserves to die..."*

[II Samuel 12:5 – ESV]

Nathan pointed out that David was that man. GOD used Nathan in order to restore King David to a right relationship with YHWH.

Everyone becomes angry at some point in their life. I imagine that everyone has also responded to that anger in appropriate and inappropriate ways. If anger invokes a reflexive response of being verbally or physically abusive, we are out of line. Anger is an intense emotion that must be controlled and expressed in a manner that will not cause harm to either party. My favorite section of scripture that provides a process for expressing our anger appropriately was written by James nearly 2,000 years ago.

> *"Know this, my beloved*
> *brothers: let every person*
> *be quick to hear, slow to*
> *speak; for the anger of*
> *man does not produce the*
> *the righteousness of God."*
> *[James 1:19,20 – ESV]*

The formula to more suitably handle our anger is outlined in these verses. Listen very carefully to the other person so that we understand exactly their perspective. Consider our response very carefully. Allow ourselves time for anger to simmer down so that we respond more logically than emotionally. The tendency is to do the exact opposite. We become angry and it controls our emotions; we then engage in a verbal barrage against the person and we simply do not take time to listen. Uncontrolled anger can result in us becoming verbally, emotionally, and physically abusive. That type of response is contrary to appropriate resolution of conflict.

I have unfortunately witnessed the damaging effects of anger being expressed inappropriately. I know a husband who became so angry with his wife that he literally broke her fingers with his bare hands. I know of another husband who allowed his anger to control him so much that he would verbally berate his wife and eventually shoved her and broke her wrist. With physical abuse there is always emotional abuse. With emotional abuse there is not always physical abuse. There should be zero tolerance for emotional or physical abuse.

The scriptures do not say: "Do not be angry". There are circumstances that legitimately make us angry. Our LORD became angry with his disciples when they were limiting the ability of children to spend time with HIM.

> *"And they were bringing children to him that he might touch them, and the disciples rebuked them. But when Jesus saw it, HE was indignant and said to them: "Let the children come to Me, do not hinder them, for to such belongs the kingdom of God. Truly, I say to you, whoever does not receive the kingdom of God like a child shall not enter it. And He took them in His arms and blessed them, laying HIS hands on them."*
> *[Mark 1013-16 – ESV]*

I do not believe there is any evidence that the disciples ever again denied children to access the LORD. They apparently learned from His rebuke. The response of our LORD is exemplary. He became angry and confronted the issue. He did not become verbally abusive to His disciples.

When my favorite daughter was fourteen years old, she asked our blessing on developing a friendship with Claudia [not her actual name]. Her mother and I were reluctant because Claudia's family had multiple issues that were very concerning. Our daughter pressured us indicating she wanted to take Claudia to church, get her involved in the youth group and interact with our family in a positive environment. My wife and I eventually agreed to a probationary type of arrangement. It became quite apparent after a few months that Claudia was very controlling and exerting a detrimental influence on our daughter. We both agreed that the relationship had to be severed completely.

Claudia's family became irate at this decision. Claudia had an eighteen-year-old brother who started hassling us. He would call at 3:00 a.m. and hang up. The next night he'd call and curse me out. He would also call and threaten me personally. This harassment continued for several weeks. I had determined basically to not respond. I might occasionally interject a 'whatever' - but did not want to make the situation more combustible. What I did not realize was that my anger was gradually building up inside of me.

Finally, I simply had enough. I've literally only been in one fight in my entire life when a man jumped me at a college football game. Late afternoon one Saturday, the phone rang and it was Claudia's brother. He was yelling, cursing and threatening me. I became so angry that I was completely calm and determined. I told him that this could end today. I challenged him to come to my house. He and a friend arrived at my house. I told my wife to lock the doors and not come outside for any reason. I grabbed my son's aluminum baseball bat and went out on my driveway. I was not exactly sure what my rights were, but I thought it would be better for them to actually be on my property. They both got out of their vehicle and continued their profanity and threats. I simply responded: "This is the day you've been waiting for - come on!!" The verbosity from these two young men continued but I remained unusually calm and determined. They taunted me by saying I was too old to handle them. I informed them that I was confidant I could get one of them and asked who'd like to come first.

My plan was simply to hit them in the knees and then call the police. I absolutely did not care if I injured them and had zero regard for my personal well-being. Thankfully, my wife called the police and they forced these guys to leave. I never heard from them again. I often ask myself, "Did I do the right thing?" My final response is, "No". What if they would have come at me and I had intended to hit their knees but one of them tripped and I hit him in the head.

That would have been a tragic outcome for both of us. I really was surprised at myself, and it frightened me to see that I was so out of control with my anger that I was calm. I share this because we all have the capability to cause harm to others when our anger consumes us. My unresolved anger had obviously been gradually stored in my emotional backpack. That anger had to be released and only by the grace of God no-one was injured.

"A Tale of Two Wolves: "One evening an old Cherokee told his grandson about a battle that goes on inside of people. He said, "My son, the battle is between two 'wolves' inside us all. One is Evil. It is anger, envy, jealousy, doubt, sorrow, regret, greed, arrogance, self-pity, guilt, resentment, inferiority, lies, false pride, superiority, and ego. The other is Good. It is joy, peace, hope, serenity, humility, kindness, benevolence, empathy, generosity, forgiveness, truth,

compassion and faith.
The grandson thought about it for a minute
and then asked his grandfather: "Which will win??"
The old Cherokee simply replied, "The one you feed."
[Credit: claritychi.com]

The apostle Paul provided a similar contrast and challenge to the believers in churches throughout Galatia.

"Now the works of the flesh
are evident: sexual immorality,
impurity, sensuality, idolatry,
sorcery, enmity, strife, jealousy,
fits of anger, rivalries, dissensions,
divisions, envy, drunkenness, orgies,
and things like these. I warn you, as
I warned you before, that those who
do such things will not inherit the
kingdom of God.
But, the fruit of the Spirit is love,
joy, peace, patience kindness,
goodness, faithfulness, gentleness,
self-control, against such things
there is no law."
[Galatians 5:19-23 – ESV].

It behooves us all to walk in a manner that is pleasing to our CREATOR. Exercise self-control in expressing your anger. Anger that is conveyed inappropriately causes harm to the marriage relationship. Do not feed anger as it can become a consuming fire that will divide and destroy.

"A soft answer turns away wrath,

but a harsh word stirs up anger."
[Proverbs 15:1 – ESV]

There are things that we do that will cause our spouse to be rightfully angry with us and vice versa. Pray without ceasing that we will express our anger in a controlled demeanor that will be honoring to our Creator.

"...for the anger of man
does not produce the
righteousness of GOD."
[James 1:20 – ESV]

Lady Nancy Astor to Winston Churchill:
"Winston, if you were my husband, I'd
Poison your tea!!!'
Churchill responded:
"Nancy, if I were your husband,
I'd drink it!!"

Listen so you can resolve, not so you can win

Listen so you can resolve, not so you can win. I have never had anyone in a counseling setting express to me that they are a perfect listener. Listening is a learned behavior that needs continual attention. Listening is giving thoughtful and deliberate attention to what the other person is saying, with the intention of understanding. "Are you listening to me?" is a common question in marriage.

Connect these dots...
Listen and Silent consist of the same letters!

I have observed the interaction of many couples in marital counseling over the last thirty-five years. Although I've never kept a statistical log, I am convinced that the majority of husbands have proven to be more inept listeners than their wives.

"...still a man hears what
he wants to hear and
disregards the rest..."
[The Boxer – 1969
Simon & Garfunkel]

When we engage a conversation that deals with conflict, our pre-conceived notions often create a barrier to truly listening to our spouse. I believe that listening is a gift that we give to each other in a marriage that demonstrates a high level of respect. We need to listen to each other to understand the other person's perspective. A barrier to listening is thinking about our next response during the time we are supposed to be listening. How do you know if your spouse is listening to you? Eye contact is essential in conveying that we are focused on listening. We also might nod our head indicating that we are 'locked in' and tracking what is being said. The cell phone has become a major deterrent to listening to each other. I have had couples in my office texting during a session dealing with conflict resolution. Another deterrent to efficacious listening is completing the other person's sentence for them. That becomes a trigger for frustration, especially if it is a frequent occurrence. Interrupting your spouse in the

middle of them expressing their concerns has the potential to frustrate and infuriate them.

If we are going to really listen, we need to put the cell phone away, put the book down, or turn off the television. Our spouse deserves our undivided attention. One proven method in demonstrating to our spouse that we are paying attention is reflective listening. If our wife is talking for a couple minutes and she asks, "Are you listening to me?", then we should be able to reflect back to her what she has been saying. This need not be a verbatim response, but a decent summarization will prove invaluable.

The ability to speak several
languages is an asset, but
the ability to keep your
mouth shut in any language
is priceless.
[Anonymous]

Think about the design of our Creator. He has equipped us with two eyes, two ears, and one mouth. Most of the time we would enhance our ability to listen if we used our eyes and ears twice as much as our mouth! We need to engage our auditory and visual senses to the maximum extent in order to enhance our listening skills.

"We have two ears
and one tongue so
that we would listen
more and talk less."
[Diogenes, 5th Century B.C.]

When conflict arises in a marriage and a discussion ensues, we must be inclined to make an honest assessment of our preconceived perspectives. The possibility exists that we are proceeding to argue with inaccurate or incomplete information. When we become aware that our perspective is erroneous, we have a choice to make that can more quickly lead to a positive outcome. We need to be willing to admit that we are wrong. We all have a propensity to not be forthcoming in admitting that we made an error in judgment. There are four powerful words that can lend to mutually beneficial outcomes: "I'm wrong" and "I'm sorry".

Pride is an obstacle to genuine communication. If we are listening and come to the realization that we are in fact wrong, be willing to admit it as soon as it become apparent.

Then if you've said or done something that was hurtful to the other person, be genuine in offering an apology.

My wife asked me earlier: "Are you listening to me?", which is really a weird way to begin a conversation.

Communication should not be considered a competition with 'winning' as the goal. If there is a perceived 'winner', there is also a perceived 'loser'. It is not a profitable outcome if our spouse comes away with a feeling that they are a 'loser'. It is far more constructive if both parties give each other the respectful gift of listening.

"One of the most sincere forms of respect is actually listening to what another

has to say."
[Bryant H. McGill]

"Most of the successful
people I have known are
the ones who do more
listening than talking."
[Barnard Baruch]

"When people talk, listen
completely. Most people
never listen."
[Ernest Hemingway]

"Most people do not listen
with the intent to understand;
they listen with the intent to
reply."
[Steven R. Covey]

Veto generalizations, boil down to specific issues

Veto generalizations, boil down to specific issues. There seems to be a propensity to respond more generally than specifically in handling conflict. Let's imagine that it is Jerry's responsibility to take out the trash on Monday evenings. His wife, Julia, has an unexpressed expectation that this task should be completed by 9:00 p.m. Jerry comes home on Monday and hurriedly makes a sandwich, gets a drink, and relaxes to enjoy Monday Night Football. He has not thought about the trash one second. It was not an intentional dereliction of duty.

Julia has had a long day and comes home about 9:30 p.m. When she enters the kitchen, she immediately notices the trash has not been emptied. This was the 'last straw' to an emotionally draining day. She bolts into the 'man cave' and confronts her husband with these emphatic words: "You are an irresponsible person!" What is Jerry supposed to do with that? He has not thought about the trash, and Julia has not mentioned the trash. He might fire back in kind with a derogatory adjective or expletive. Or he may choose to 'bunker in' and hope that the verbal attack dissipates so that he can return to the ball game. Because of the general nature of Julia's initial interaction, it is possible to have a full-blown argument and half the parties involved have no idea what the real issue is. If the trash is the issue, stay focused on the trash being emptied. In this hypothetical situation, Julia chose to attack the person and not the problem. She made a very general characterization of Jerry as a person. Communication can be greatly enhanced if we are determined to be as specific as possible. Broad characterizations are impractical to deal with by practical actions. If we maintain a laser focus on a specific issue, then practical expectations and outcomes become more apparent.

Explore your options for reaching both of your goals

Explore your options to reach both of your goals. One of my goals in counseling is to facilitate good communication that will result in conflict resolution. There have been numerous sessions where I have questioned whether the husband and wife truly want to resolve issues. I challenge couples to accept the goal of fervently wanting to resolve the conflicts that they are experiencing. When conflict becomes discernable, I encourage couples to make a mental determination to answer this simple question: "What can I do to make this better?" If both the husband and wife develop this foundational viewpoint, then they can experience reciprocity that will provide vitality to effectuate conflict resolution.

On August 11, 2021, a 28 ounce
piece of Princess Diana's 1981
wedding cake was sold at auction
for $2500.00.
The wedding cake of Prince and
Princess of Wales had five tiers,
was five feet tall, and weighed
two hundred and twenty-five
pounds.
[US Magazine / Royals 07/29/21
And 08/11/21]

Discipline yourself to stay on the topic

Discipline yourself to stay on the topic. This is a reiteration of 'Veto gener-
alizations, boil down to specific issues'. It takes mental discipline to remain
specifically focused on resolving the issue at hand. We have a proclivity
to pancake other issues on top of the current problem. These issues can be
retrieved from our memory banks concerning past conflicts that we were
not satisfactorily resolved. It is far more productive to remain disciplined
and focus on the issue at hand.

To reiterate:

> ➢ *Remember to attack the problem, not the person*

> ➢ *Escaping the problem does not solve it*

> ➢ *Speak the truth in love*

➢ *Out of control is out of line*

➢ *Listen so you can resolve, not so you can win*

➢ *Explore your options for reaching both your goals*

➢ *Discipline yourself to stay on the topic*

"The 3 C's of Life:
Choices, Chances, Changes
You must make the choice,
to take a chance, if you want
anything in life to change."
[Zig Ziglar]

Make the determination early in the resolution of conflict to do what you can to make the situation better. We need to examine ourselves accurately and determine what changes we need to make first. Be proactive as you demonstrate the genuine desire to be a peacemaker.

Clementine, Sir Winston's wife,
was talking to a street sweeper for
a while.
"What did you talk about for
so long?" asked Sir Winston.
She smiled, "Many years ago
He was madly in love with me."
Churchill smiled ironically,
"So you could have been the wife
Of a street sweeper today."

*"Oh no, my love", Clementine
Replied, "If I had married him,
he would have been the prime
minister today."
[William Poutu – Facebook
Post – 08/15/2021]*

*Remember, behind every successful
man is a surprised mother-in-law!*

Forgiveness and Repentance

*"Put on then, as God's chosen ones, holy and
beloved, compassionate hearts, kindness, humility,
meekness, patience, bearing with one another and,
if one has a complaint against another, forgiving each other;
as the LORD has forgiven you, so you must forgive."
[Colossians 3:12,13 – ESV]*

*"Let all bitterness and wrath and anger and clamor and
slander be put away from you, along with all malice. Be kind
to one another, tenderhearted, forgiving one another, as God
in Christ forgave you."
[Ephesians 4:31,32 – ESV]*

*As believers, because we have been forgiven by GOD – we need to be
forgiving. The ability to forgive is a characteristic that enables us to be
ambassadors for the LORD.*

Unresolved anger transforms into resentment and bitterness. Bitterness will produce a harvest of destruction. If you are unwilling to forgive your spouse, you invite injurious consequences into your life and your marriage.

"Resentment [bitterness] is like taking poison and waiting for the other person to die."
[Malachy McCourt]

A practical scriptural definition of forgiveness is that you no longer hold the offense against the person. I often hear people respond that forgiveness means to 'forgive and forget'.

That is a challenging concept for us as human beings. The scripture indicates that GOD has the ability to forgive and choose not to call our offenses into HIS memory.

"For as high as the heavens are above the earth, so great is HIS steadfast love toward those who fear him; as far as the east is from the west, so far does HE remove our transgressions from us."
[Psalm 103:11,12 – ESV]

"HE will again have compassion on us; HE will tread our iniquities underfoot. YOU will cast all our sins into the depths of the sea."
[Micah 7:19 – ESV]

127

"For I will forgive their
iniquity, and I will remember
their sin no more."
[Jeremiah 31:34 – ESV]

"Blessed are those whose
lawless deeds are forgiven,
and whose sins are covered;
blessed is the man against
whom the LORD will not
count his sin."
[Romans 4:7,8 – ESV]

On November 1, 1997, Charles and Marie Roberts became the proud parents of their first daughter, Elsie. No doubt they had been looking forward to her birth with great anticipation for months. Complications arose and Elsie was born three months prematurely.

Elsie was only able to cling to life for twenty minutes and she died. Charles became angry at GOD over the loss of his daughter. He allowed his anger to turn into bitterness and this condition festered for nine years.

On October 2, 2006, Charles called his wife with a disturbing message that he would not be returning home. Marie had absolutely no idea of what Charles was about to do. The thought entered her mind that he was going to take his own life. She reported later that Charles had conveyed to her that he was 'getting back at the LORD'. Charles entered the West Nickel Mines School in Lancaster, Pennsylvania. This was an Old Order Amish one-room schoolhouse. He instructed the male students to leave. Charles took ten young Amish girls as hostages and terrorized them over the next thirty-two minutes. Charles shot eight Amish girls and five of them succumbed to their wounds. He subsequently committed suicide.

The leader of the Old Order Amish proceeded to lead by example in an incredible practical lesson about forgiveness and reconciliation. The Amish were making a deliberate and willful choice to forgive the perpetrator. Neighbors immediately approached the father of Charles Roberts as they recognized he was also a victim and in extreme shock and disbelief.

These neighbors consoled him and ministered to him in multiple ways to assist him in dealing with this unspeakable tragedy.

When the day came to bury Charles Roberts, several members of the Amish community decided to attend his funeral. These folks embraced Marie and other family members recognizing their need for individual and community support. They chose to demonstrate unconditional love and empathy, instead of a judgmental attitude. Members of the community brought food to the Roberts home. The Amish collected money to present to Mrs. Roberts and her children.

The Amish leadership decided to destroy the schoolhouse where the murders occurred.

A new schoolhouse was built, and they chose the name: New Hope School. The midwife who delivered many of the girls killed and injured was interviewed by an NBC News reporter. She was asked: "How is forgiveness possible?" The midwife responded with a profound truth:

"This is possible if you have the love of Christ in your heart!!" The Amish community fervently believed that the only possible way to deal with the enormous hurt and grief was to pursue the path of forgiveness. The Amish gained the attention and respect of the nation as they became living instruments to apply the balm of forgiveness to hurting souls.

Even when we are hurt in our marriage relationship healing is possible through the powerful concept of forgiveness. Forgiveness is therapeutically beneficial to the offended party and the offending party. Forgiveness can be a moment in time, or a process and it is always worth pursuing. Forgiveness is an essential component of truly resolving conflict.

Forgiveness is not often easily achieved. Incidents of moral failure, adultery, or abuse are exceptionally onerous. If adultery impacts the marriage that is one of the most difficult offenses to forgive. I've heard wives express the mental images that consume their thoughts.

Their self-esteem is crushed and trust for their husband is devastated.

I am required to take a certain number of continuing education hours every year in order to maintain my counseling license. On June 9, 2000, I attended a marriage seminar on the campus of West Virginia University. The presenter was a noted 'specialist' in the field of marriage counseling and possessed a Doctorate in Philosophy. I utilize the triangle diagram in many of my counseling sessions and seminars because it is the strongest multi-sided figure known to man. The triangle provides an excellent format for visualization of concepts. The doctor piqued my interest when he announced to the seventy counselors in attendance that he used a triangle diagram in his counseling sessions. He then proceeded to draw an equilateral triangle on his overhead presentation. On one side of the triangle, he wrote 'HUSBAND' and on another side he wrote 'WIFE'. On the remaining third side he wrote the word 'AFFAIR'.

He then attempted to develop a case indicating that an affair was good for the marriage. He postulated that becoming involved in an affair and bringing a third person into the marriage for a brief period of time, would strengthen the marriage. It was one of the most bizarre training sessions that I have attended. What intrigued me even more was the fact that many counselors listening to him were nodding in agreement. Adultery destroys trust and is never beneficial. Adultery is one of the most difficult things to forgive and recover from in the Covenant of Marriage.

A wife from a rural county in my home state of West Virginia was married to a man who was a serial adulterer. She has caught him on numerous occasions and in fact he does not make any real effort to hide his promiscuity. It is unimaginable to me that he claims to be a Christian and yet continues his adulterous activity. It is enigmatic to me that she has made the determination to stay with him despite his widely known infidelity. Most of the time when adultery impacts a marriage the offended person may possibly forgive and restore the marriage once. But a second offense usually results in divorce.

Caterpillars are amazing creatures in the design of our Creator. Caterpillars undergo a fascinating transformation in the process of metamorphosis. The caterpillar discontinues eating and then attaches itself upside down to a leaf or limb. In an amazing act of transformation, the caterpillar weaves itself into a protective casing and will eventually emerge as a butterfly or moth. The caterpillar has realized a complete change in its physical structure and has become what God intended it to become. Metamorphosis is a change in the physical structure.

Repentance is an English word which originated from the Greek language. The word of origin in the Greek language is 'metanoia'. Metanoia literally means to 'change one's mind'. It can also mean a complete 'change of heart'. I often ask counselees to define repentance and I obtain some interesting responses. One common response is that repentance is a '360-degree turn'. Let's imagine you are traveling down a road. This road is paved with bad choices, immoral choices, or unwise choices. The scripture relates that there is pleasure in sin for a season [Hebrews 11:25], but that season of pleasure always expires. If a person is desirous of getting off that road and repenting, they cannot achieve that by completing a '360-degree turn'. Turning 360 degrees will result in them being on the same dead-end pavement. True repentance, metanoia, is to change your mind completely.

You've got to realize that the road you are traveling is eventually leading to a disastrous destination. True repentance is in reality a '180- degree turn'.

In the Hebrew language the word for repentance is 'teshuva'. "Teshuva' conveys a two-fold aspect of repentance. There is a turning away from the unwise or evil choices and a turning to God. We can then turn to God and start doing those things that are acceptable and pleasing in HIS sight. The determination to truly repent, empowered by YHWH, will completely change our lives. The best way to prove to your spouse that you are sorry is to truly repent. Stop engaging in the hurtful activity. In the case of adultery, the offended party can choose to forgive, but it is the offending party who must demonstrate repentance.

I had the opportunity to work with a couple several years ago. The wife had become unfaithful to her husband. The husband became aware of the adultery and was willing to forgive. However, his wife refused to accept responsibility for her immoral choice. She was blaming her husband for 'causing' her to become unfaithful. She developed a stance where she continually projected blame rather than accept responsibility. True repentance is when a person admits they are wrong in the sight of God and their spouse and asks for forgiveness. Then they pursue a walk in their life that proves they can be trusted and remain faithful from that point on. The wife mentioned above thought that it was her husband's responsibility to pursue her in such a way that she would remain faithful. It was a perspective that eventually resulted in them divorcing. She really never repented and did not discontinue her unfaithfulness.

Forgiveness is not 'evening the score'. I worked with a lady whose husband was unfaithful to her. I believe she became engulfed in spiritual warfare and the enemy was profoundly tempting her. She was considering committing adultery to 'balance the scales' so that her husband would know exactly the amount of hurt she had experienced. One can never do wrong and expect that will produce a positive outcome. Thankfully, she chose to forgive and engage in the process of restoration. Her husband acknowledged his sin and took complete responsibility. He repented and they were able to restore their marriage. They renewed their vows and even exchanged new wedding rings which was indicative of a fresh start in their covenant of marriage.

A willingness to forgive the offending party is vital in restoration. Demonstrating an unwavering persistence to remain on the path of repentance is absolutely indispensable to rebuild trust and to reestablish the bond of intimacy.

> *"Above all, love each*
> *other deeply, because*
> *love covers a multitude*
> *of sins."*
> *[I Peter 4:8 – NIV]*

A caring touch enhances the level of intimacy for a couple. The touch being referenced here is not sexual in nature. It is a touch that conveys you are emotionally connected. A kindhearted embrace or holding of the hand produces feelings of assurance.

These positive feelings transmit and solidify the foundational needs of significance and security. A caring touch seems to be more prevalent during the dating times. Once the couple marries, there seems to be a tendency for this type of touching to diminish. This is a gradual 'drifting away' process. If we do not continue to touch each other in this manner, we start to subconsciously question if we are significant to our spouse and secure in the marriage relationship. Touch probably is the most critical non-verbal communication available for us to share. A caring touch assists in relieving stress and brings a sense of calm to the situation.

There are multiple components that constitute intimacy. One of those components is building positive memories that allow you to glance back at the blessings YHWH has allowed in our lives and marriages. The nation of Israel spent 430 years in Egypt and for a large portion of that time they were enslaved. YHWH delivered Israel from the bondage of Egypt utilizing ten object lessons [more commonly referred to as the Ten Plagues] that were designed to challenge the 'gods' of Egypt. Israel witnessed YHWH part the Red Sea and that miracle enabled Israel to begin an extraordinary journey to their Promised Land. It was time to cross into the Land of Promise and receive their national inheritance. YHWH, in effect, recreated the parting of the Red Sea when He allowed Israel to cross the Jordan River on dry ground.

Israel was instructed by Joshua to take twelve stones from the Jordan and erect a monument at Gilgal. These were "Stones of Remembrance" that would encourage Israel to recall the blessings that YHWH had imparted to them. This stone monument would be a sign to future generations of the goodness of YHWH. I think it is essential to make the effort to erect 'Stones of Remembrance' in our marriages. These memories can vary as to magnitude but pay enormous dividends over the long haul. A most efficacious way of improving intimacy and erecting these 'Stones of Remembrance' is to invest time with each other. Troubles are more inclined to increase if a couple does not make a dedicated effort to put each other on the calendar. I often hear a recurring request, mostly from wives, that refers to their desire to spend more time with their husband. During the dating process, we normally don't have much difficulty in making time for each other. Investing time and continuing to date are often neglected after the exchange of vows.

*I just asked my husband if he remembered
what today is...scaring men is easy.
[Credit: 'OneLineFun']*

The Good Wife's Guide – [appeared in Housekeeping Monthly – May 13, 1955]

➢ *Have dinner ready. Plan ahead, even the night before, to have a delicious meal ready, on time for his return. This is a way of letting him know that you have been thinking about him and are concerned about his needs. Most men are hungry when they come home, and the prospect of a good meal (especially his favorite dish) is part of the warm welcome needed.*

➢ *Prepare yourself. Take fifteen minutes to rest so you'll be refreshed when he arrives. Touch up your make-up, put a ribbon in your hair and be fresh-looking. He has just been with a lot of work-weary people.*

➢ *Be a little gay and a little more interesting for him. His boring day may need a lift and one of your duties is to provide it.*

➢ *Clear away the clutter. Make one last trip through the main part of the house just before your husband arrives.*

➢ *Gather up schoolbooks, toys, paper, etc. and then run a dust cloth over the tables.*

➢ *Over the cooler months of the year, you should prepare and light a fire for him to unwind by. Your husband will feel he has reached a haven of rest and order, and it will give you a lift too. After all, catering for his comfort will provide you with immense personal satisfaction.*

➢ *Prepare the children. Take a few minutes to wash the children's hands and faces [if they are small], comb their hair and, if necessary, change their clothes. They are little treasures and he would like to see them playing the part. Minimize all noise. At the time of his arrival, eliminate all noise of the washer, dryer or vacuum. Try to encourage the children to be quiet.*

➢ *Be happy to see him.*

➢ *Greet him with a warm smile and show sincerity in your desire to please.*

➢ *Listen to him. You may have a dozen important things to tell him, but the moment of his arrival is not the time. Let him talk first – remember, his topics of conversation are more important than yours.*

➢ *Make the evening his. Never complain if he comes home late or goes out to dinner, or other places of entertainment without you. Instead, try to understand his world of strain and pressure and his very real need to be at home and relax.*

➢ *Your goal: Try to make sure your home is a place of peace, order, and tranquility where your husband can renew himself in body and spirit.*

➢ *Don't greet him with complaints and problems.*

➢ *Don't complain if he's late home for dinner or even if he stays out all night. Count this as minor compared to what he might have gone through that day.*

> *Make him comfortable. Have him lean back in a comfortable chair or have him lie down in the bedroom. Have a cool or warm drink ready for him.*

> *Arrange his pillow and offer to take off his shoes. Speak in a low, soothing and pleasant voice.*

> *Don't ask him questions about his actions or question his judgment or integrity. Remember, he is the master of the house and as such, will always exercise his will with fairness and truthfulness. You have no right to question him.*

> *A good wife always knows her place.*

I would really like to know who authored this 'guide'. If it was authored by a man, he had to be the most chauvinistic man on the planet. If it was written by a woman, she had to be naïve, abused, or lacked a great deal of self-esteem. Take a moment to consider this perspective. Do you know any man who expects this type of treatment? The truth be known, there are still a significant number of chauvinistic men who would be supportive of this 'guide'...SMH!!!

XXXXXXXXXXXXXXXXXXXXXXXXXXXXXXXXXXXXXXXXXXXXXXX
XXXXXXXXXXXXXXXXXXXXXXXXXXXXXXXXXXXXXXXXXXXXXXX

My wife, Deanna, and I met at Fairmont State College in Fairmont, West Virginia. We spent time playing cards and talking with each other in the 'Nickel', which was the student socialization area. Our first actual date was traveling with her parents, Jim and Nina, about an hour north to watch Salem College play basketball against Waynesburg College in Pennsylvania. Her brother, Jim, played for Salem College. On other dates, we enjoyed meals at some local restaurants and occasionally went to the movies. On our 10th anniversary I decided to put together an album of our college memories. I drove to Waynesburg, PA and took a picture of the gymnasium and the seats where our first date occurred. I took pictures of the "Nickel", various restaurants and the movie theater, etc. I assembled these photographs in an album and my bride still has that album. These were positive "Stones of Remembrance" during the early formation of our relationship.

We enjoyed spending time together dancing and our favorite song was 'Color My World' by Chicago. Approximately thirty years ago, I had a friend print the words of this song in old English script and had it framed. We even had the opportunity to see Chicago perform in concert. We still have that framed artwork.

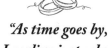

"As time goes by,
I realize just what
you mean to me.
And now, now that
you're near,
Promise your love
that I've waited to
share.
And dreams of our
moments together,
color my world with
hope of loving you."
[Chicago –
Color My World
1970]

Deanna is an excellent teacher and invested thirty-four years in teaching students at the Elementary and Middle School levels. On the last day

of school in the early 1990's, I surprised her with a "Summer Survival Kit". I had typed out multiple coupons that she could 'cash in' during her summer break. One coupon would pay for someone to clean the house.

Another coupon was for dinner at our favorite eating establishment - Jim Reid's Restaurant.

Other coupons included a trip to Dairy Queen, an evening in Pittsburgh, a cash coupon for $25.00, and other date nights. Only one of the coupons was reusable. I laminated the coupon that said: "Good for Passion - Anytime"!!!

Our 25th wedding anniversary was on December 30, 1997. I really wanted to surprise my bride and thankfully was able to accomplish that goal. I reserved Fellowship Bible Church, our home church, for the celebration and renewal of our vows. I invited the entire wedding party. The event was catered and many of our close friends were able to join us for this milestone celebration. I had her wedding gown cleaned and placed on a mannequin. I collected several newspaper clippings and photos from December 30, 1972. I had some special emerald jewelry crafted for her. We dressed up under the pretense of going to a surprise birthday party of a close friend. When we arrived at the church, and I opened the door to the reception room, she saw her bridal gown and heard the song, "Color My World" playing. I will never forget the look on her face and the tears of joy that swelled up in her eyes. Pastor Chris Campbell officiated in the renewal of our vows. We are now on the verge of celebrating our 50th wedding anniversary. I'll have to start planning!

We took special trips, invested in family vacations, shared dinners, enjoyed movies, and time with friends. We were quite fortunate to have several couples close to our age with whom we could fellowship. All these have become part of our collective memory – special 'Stones of Remembrance'.

As we age together, we have concluded, that between the two of us we have a complete memory!

It is crucial to continue to erect 'Stones of Remembrance' in our marriage so that the relationship does not become stagnant. One of the definitions of agape love that is included in I Corinthians 13:4 is: "Love is kind". It is nice to speak kindly to one another, but this term is more action oriented. This type of kindness is expressed by doing things with and for the other person that we know they would appreciate. On Tuesday evenings I play tennis indoors during the winter. On my way home I often stop by Krogers and purchase a bouquet of flowers for my wife. There is no special occasion involved. I spontaneously do this to let her know I love her and am thinking about her. It is often around 9:30 p.m. when I buy the flowers and I often get this response from the cashier: "Are you in trouble?"

Reciprocity in extending acts of kindness is a requisite for maturing intimacy in our marriages. An overriding consideration is that you do not 'keep score'. It will not prove to be expedient for a husband to make this determination: "I've done three really kind things lately and my wife must 'catch up' before I do any more." That perspective will lead to frustration and stifle the dynamic of intimacy. Spontaneity in expressing our love to our spouse refreshes the marriage.

Exchanging tokens of affection are practical ways of demonstrating kindness and sweetening intimacy. My wife and I were married on December 30, 1972. My wedding ring was engraved with multiple interconnected circles. Over the last forty-eight years these circles have rubbed off and are now barely distinguishable. One the inside of my ring I had inscribed the date: 12/30/1972. I thought when I got older, I might have to refer to the inscription to be sure of the exact date. Thankfully, so far, I have not had to look at the inscription to remind me of the date we said, "I do" to each other. I am amazed, in the initial session for marriage counseling, how many husbands do not remember the date of their marriage. I think it is foremost to remember and commemorate the anniversary of entering the covenant of marriage.

Other important days to exchange tokens of affection include birthdays, Valentine's Day, Christmas and your wedding anniversary. These are days on our calendar that should become reflexive times to express our love to our spouse in tangible ways. These special days only amount to a handful of days in a calendar year. If you desire to keep the romantic spark kindled in your marriage, then be mindful of other opportunities to spontaneously display your love. We have a tendency to be much more romantically spontaneous during the dating time. If this has become lacking in your marriage, now is the time to reignite the flame.

In order to maintain and improve the intimacy element of our marriage we must be intentional. If you asked my wife to grade me in the area of intimacy in the first five years of our marriage, I believe I would have garnered a "C". If you asked her to grade me after those first five years, I think she would rate me at an "A" or "B+" most of the time. The reason for this change came from my counseling experiences. I discovered that a significant portion of troubled marriages were the result of not being intentional in meeting essential intimacy needs. When this component is lacking then our spouses doubt how significant they really are to us.

*"The most important thing
a father can do for his children
is to love their mother."
[Theodore Hesburgh]*

Intimacy requires us to express unconditional positive regard for the well-being of our spouse. The Hebrew word "Shalom" is translated into English as "Peace". One of the names used by Gideon to help us understand

the character of GOD is YHWH-Shalom, the GOD of Peace. The 'peace' sign was prominently displayed on college campuses in the 1970s and often used to say 'hi' or 'bye'. But the actual meaning is profoundly more significant.

> *"Now may the God of peace Himself*
> *sanctify you completely, and may your*
> *your whole spirit and soul and body be*
> *kept blameless at the coming of our*
> *LORD JESUS CHRIST."*
> *[I Thessalonians 5:23 – ESV]*

Paul wrote these words of encouragement 2,000 years ago to the believers worshipping at the church in Thessaloniki. Thessaloniki is located in modern day Greece, and I have had the opportunity to explore the 1st century archaeological remains. Paul refers to God as the "God of peace". God's desire is for us to be sanctified, set apart for His purpose. If we believe that God exists, it is imperative that we develop a relationship with Him and allow Him to instruct us as to how we should live our lives. That instruction is explicitly recorded in the scriptures – the Original Testament and the New Testament.

Based upon the truth in this verse, we all have a trifold existence – body, soul, and spirit. God inspired Paul to employ three distinct Greek words in this verse that define our reality as humans. The Greek word used in this section of scripture for body is 'soma'. The Greek word used for soul is 'psyche' and the Greek word for spirit is 'pneuma'. It is incumbent on us to develop and maintain this trichotomy in order to achieve shalom.

Husbands and wives should work together in strengthening each of these three components of their existence. If a couple is intentional in bolstering these areas together, intimacy will be positively impacted.

We all have a body that we should maintain and care for at a high level. We need to care for our soma with good nutrition and exercise. We can choose to pursue a path of wisdom by not ingesting poisons into our soma. In the 17th century, Sir Isaac Newton formulated his Laws of Motion. One of his laws, inertia, is basically that a body at rest tends to stay at rest, and a body in motion tends to stay in motion. Humans need to keep their bodies moving. Couples can promote healthy lifestyles by being involved in regular exercise individually and as a couple. Being physically healthy contributes immensely to our emotional health. Taking good care of our personal physical health, and demonstrating concern for the health of our spouse promotes intimacy.

The second component of our trichotomy of existence is the soul. The Greek word for soul is 'psyche'. It is the derivative of the word psychology or psychological. There are two broad components of our psyche that I like to focus on in counseling. There is the intellectual component and the emotional component. It is crucial to continue to focus on exercising the intellectual portion of our lives. We need to exercise our minds just like we need to exercise our bodies. We need to put down the cell phone, turn off the television and read. Find things that challenge you to think, critically analyze, and problem solve. Actively engage your intellectual capabilities and avoid mind-numbing activities. Intellectual stimulation will help us think more clearly and focus on matters of life that are truly consequential.

Another element in our psyche is the emotional component. The overriding scriptural principle is that we are to express our emotions and not let them control us. If we are going to be controlled by one emotion, let that emotion be love for one another. Expressing our emotions was previously discussed in the conflict resolution section earlier. It is mutually beneficial for couples to promote positive intellectual and emotional health for each other.

Another significant component in the intimacy side of the covenant of marriage is caring for yourself and helping your spouse care for themselves.

"But when the Pharisees
heard that He had silenced
the Sadducees, they gathered
together. And one of them, a
lawyer, asked Him a question
to test him. "Teacher, which is the
greatest commandment in the
Law?" And He said to him,
"You shall love the LORD
your God with all your heart
and with all your soul and
and with all your mind. This
is the great and first
commandment. And a second
is like it: "You shall love your
neighbor as yourself. On these
two commandments depend all
the Law and the Prophets."
[Matthew 22:34-40 – ESV]

The scriptures mentioned above focus on the need for healthy self-care. Included in the self-care is possessing a sound level of self-esteem. We need to care for ourselves physically, emotionally, and spiritually. Equally important is motivating our spouse to do the same. If our spouse lacks an appropriate level of self-esteem; they can experience multiple symptoms. Our spouse can exhibit excessively high self-esteem to the point of pride and arrogance and that is certainly not healthy. This can cause the person to believe they are always right. They have little genuine interest in the opinion of others. They tend to be condescending, rude and excessively extroverted. Narcissism is unhealthy and highly detrimental to the marriage relationship. Unfortunately, narcissism is rampant in our society and has a deleterious effect on marriages. A healthy marriage is a partnership that focuses on the well-being of the other person. Once again, the principle of reciprocity needs to be operational.

On the other end of the continuum is low self-esteem. If our spouse has developed low self-esteem, this is manifested in a variety of behaviors. This type of person has a predisposition for depression that is typified by isolation, insecurity and inactivity. They experience anxiety in many social settings. They lack confidence and are intimidated by taking even minimal risks and motivation can be non-existent.

We need to be personally responsible for a healthy level of self-care. If that is a problem for our spouse, we need to reach out and assist them in addressing these issues. We really cannot be as effective in helping others, including our spouses, if we are not caring for ourselves in a relevant manner.

> *"For by the grace given*
> *to me I say to everyone*
> *among you not to think*
> *of himself more highly*
> *than he ought to think*
> *with sober judgment…"*
> *[Romans 12:3 – ESV]*

The third component of our trichotomous existence is the spiritual aspect. The Greek word Paul was inspired to use for spirit is 'pneuma'. Pneuma means 'breath'. YHWH fashioned a soma from the dust of the ground in Genesis 2. That 'soma' was not alive until YHWH 'breathed' the breath of life into Adam. Rosh Hashanah is when the Jews celebrate the New Year. In the Original Testament this time is referred to as the Feast of Trumpets. It is a day to blow the shofar in Jerusalem and in synagogues throughout the world. The blowing of the shofar commemorates the breathing of the breath of life into Adam. YHWH summoned Adam to life with that first breath. As humans we all possess that first breath of life. On September 6, 2021, the blowing of the shofar will introduce the year 5782 on the Jewish Calendar. Jews believe that YHWH created Adam 5,782 years ago. The blowing of the shofar is a yearly reminder to evaluate our relationship with God. The sounding of the shofar is a call for spiritual 'rebirth' and 'renewal'. As God breathed physical life into Adam, His desire is to breathe spiritual life into our existence. If we ignore the spiritual component of our existence, we lose focus of the eternal nature of life. Life is a continuum and the location of where our life is to be lived depends upon the relationship we have with our Creator.

Our Creator desires to be our Redeemer and our Sustainer.

"So God created man in His own image, in the image of God, HE created him; male and female HE created them."
[Genesis 1:27 – ESV]
[CREATOR]

"And there is salvation in no one else, for there is no other name under heaven given among men by which we must be saved."
[Acts 4:12 – ESV]

"For everyone who calls on the name of the LORD will be saved." [Romans 10:13 – ESV]
[REDEEMER]

"For by Him all things were created, in heaven and on earth, visible and invisible, whether thrones or dominions or rulers or authorities – all things were created through Him and for Him. And He is before all things, and in Him

all things hold together."
[Colossians 1:16,17 – ESV]
[SUSTAINER]

One of the most effective ways to improve intimacy is to invest quality and quantity time with each other. I coached the Liberty Christian Academy Girls' Tennis Team. We spent a significant amount of time together practicing and playing actual matches. I regularly shared scriptural devotions with them. As we neared the end of the season, I shared with these fine young ladies an important truth: 'The greatest gift that we can give to another person is investing time with them." I told them I appreciated the time that they invested for the team. It was a blessing for me to be their coach. The same principle is critical in improving the intimacy component of the Covenant of Marriage. We all have the exact same amount of time – twenty-four hours per day. How we invest our time demonstrates what we value. We can positively improve our intimacy levels if we demonstrate how much we value our spouse by investing time with them. The more time we invest with our spouse the more intimate we become. The more intimacy we experience cements the emotional bonding more securely.

'And no, you can't fence time
And you can't stop love.
["Suds in the Bucket"
Sara Evans – 2003]

[One of the best ways to
improve the level of intimacy
in the marriage is to invest
time with one another.]

Adam was not an illiterate Neanderthal. Adam was intelligent and artic- ulate. Adam possessed the capability of knowing YHWH and developing a relationship with Him.

Humans are the only portion of the creation of YHWH that knows YHWH exists. We can knowingly choose to develop a relationship with YHWH and worship Him. The lack of spiritual agreement in a marriage can be a major source of stress.

> *"Do not be unequally yoked with unbelievers. For what partnership has righteousness with lawlessness?"*
> *[II Corinthians 6:14]*

One major source of contention in a marriage can easily be avoided if the couple pays close attention to the advice the Apostle Paul gave to the church at Corinth. Do not be unequally yoked. Another way of defining this terminology is for the couple to be spiritually 'likeminded'. If you are a disciple of YESHUA, you should seek out a spouse who is also a disciple. I have witnessed the turmoil that is caused by a Christian marrying a non-Christian.

I have counseled with women prior to marriage who were dating a non-believer. They were naively mistaken that they could get their man converted after the marriage. I will not say that conversion after mar- riage is impossible, but it is not the norm. In general, what you see during the dating time is what you will experience after the exchange of vows. "Missionary Marriages" are a risky proposition at best. It is far more ben- eficial to be of one mind and in one accord spiritually as you enter the Covenant of Marriage. I acknowledge and believe that complete change is possible at any point in our lives if we make that decision to follow Christ.

One way that a couple can improve the intimacy area of their marriage is to minister together or encourage one another to be involved in opportunities to serve and minister to other people. Paul wrote words of challenge and encouragement to believers in the churches throughout the region of Galatia.

> *"And let us not grow*
> *weary of doing good,*
> *for in due season we*
> *will reap, if we do not*
> *give up. So then, as we*
> *have opportunity, let us*
> *do good to everyone, and*
> *especially those who are*
> *of the household of faith."*
> *[Galatians 6:9,10]*

Couples who are involved in helping others realize a terrific amount of personal satisfaction and a sense of fulfillment. Projects that the couple can do together are an excellent investment of time. In the 1980s my wife and I started the Youth Program at Fellowship Bible Church in Bridgeport, WV. We were able to coordinate many activities for the kids and it was a terrific blessing to minister together in that effort. For many years we hosted a home Bible study which I led, and Deanna provided the hospitality.

We have worked together in supporting various ministries with the income that GOD has allowed us to earn. In complete agreement, we have supported multiple individuals with Campus Crusade for Christ, purchased a motorcycle for a Pastor in the Philippines, paid for the sign language translation of the Book of Nehemiah for individuals who are deaf, raised money to build two houses for a village in Guatemala, sent our granddaughter, Violet, on mission trips to Guatemala and helped

*friends and family in need financially. My wife and I recently volun-
teered at a local food bank packaging various food items. These packages
are then delivered to local schools for distribution on Friday afternoons
so that children in need have food for the weekends.*

*I want to encourage my wife to grow closer to YHWH and she does the
same for me. I encourage her to participate in Bible studies, and go to
seminars with groups of ladies [like Extraordinary Women Conferences].
Deanna has been a terrific source of support and encouragement to me in
various ministry opportunities. Due to her support and encouragement,
I began teaching for Walk Thru the Bible Ministries headquartered in
Atlanta, GA. A co-worker of mine had participated in a WTB seminar
in Morgantown, WV.*

*She was part of our home Bible study. She was excited about the six-
hour Old Testament Seminar and told me she was positive I would enjoy
attending the seminar and that she could see me teaching these types of
seminars. I read over the material and watched a video and was intrigued
about this teaching ministry. I wrote the President of WTB, Dr. Bruce
Wilkinson, asking what I would need to do to become a WTB Instructor.
I received a reply with about twelve needed qualifications. The first one
on the list was that one had to have graduated from seminary. I felt I
met all the other eleven qualifications, but was discouraged by the first
requirement. A couple of weeks later, I reread the letter and discussed it
with Deanna. She encouraged me to write a follow-up letter indicating
that I felt I met all the expected criteria except one. After we discussed this
situation further, I did write a letter and asked Dr. Wilkinson to send me
a doctrinal questionnaire that I could complete and submit. If my answers
were doctrinally sound, I asked for the opportunity to participate in the
training. He accepted my answers to the questionnaire and had his father,
Jim Wilkinson, contact my Pastor for a recommendation. I was invited
to come to Atlanta for the Old Testament training in June of 1987. I
completed the training for the Old Testament, and was later trained in*

teaching the New Testament and other seminars. I have been blessed to conduct nearly 300 seminars for WTB. I have taught in fifteen states and Washington, DC. I represented WTB on mission trips to Estonia, St. Petersburg, Moscow, Siberia, Albania, and Bulgaria. This required me to be away from home quite a significant amount of time. This would not have been possible without the consistent encouragement from Deanna. She was always with me by prayer and encouragement.

There are multiple ways for couples to minister together. It can be through a church, community organization or just looking for ways to help other people. In my opinion, there is a terrific therapeutic value for couples to be involved in ministry and support ministries together. Ministering together is an effective way to positively impact the intimacy side of the covenant of marriage.

I also applied this principle of being 'equally yoked' to my counseling prac-tice. My first private counseling office was located at 113 State Street, Bridgeport, WV. I advertised quite openly that I would be providing counseling utilizing scriptural principles and praying with my clients. In the same office complex, just four doors down from me, was a group of counselors. There was the owner of the business and a husband-and-wife team sharing the office space. Immediately after I moved in and started seeing clients their office began distributing pamphlets indicating that they provided counseling without any 'God-Talk', Bible referencing, or praying. Within a couple of months, the husband-and-wife team left that practice. The owner called me and wanted me to consider moving into her office in order to share expenses. I politely declined the offer because we would have obviously been 'unequally yoked'.

If the couple who enters the Covenant of Marriage is 'equally yoked' they invite the blessings of YHWH into their home. The like-mindedness that they have as a spiritual foundation will impact all areas of decision making. Being harmonious in the spiritual side of life is one way to ensure a healthy approach to parenting.

No marriage is perfect. No marriage is free from stress. Caleb and Candra Pence of Harper County, Kansas had made plans for an outdoor wedding ceremony on May 19, 2012.

Caleb is a bull rider and Candra is a rodeo barrel racer. They also live in "Tornado Alley" and invested time together chasing tornadoes on occasion. They hired the services of photographer Cate Eighmey to capture their special day. As the couple exchanged vows next to a field of wheat, tornadoes touched down in the distance behind them. The photos taken by Eighmey went viral on the internet. This Kansas cowboy and his lady weathered the storms that day and completed their entry into the covenant of marriage. Take a moment to view these pictures on the internet.

[Credit to "The Wichita Eagle", article: 'Tornadoes make appearance in Kansas couple's wedding photos, by Stan Finger, May 22, 2012.]

> *"I have said these things to you, that in Me you may have peace. In the world you will have tribulations. But take heart; I have overcome the world."*
> *[John 16:33 – ESV]*

The pictures of the tornado in the background serve as a reminder of the fact that trials and tribulation will be experienced in a marriage. The couple is much more likely to weather the storms of life together if they share a common faith in the LORD.

I initially became aware of a man by the name of Sullivan Ballou when I watched the Ken Burns documentary series on the Civil War in 1990. Sullivan was born on March 28, 1829, in Smithfield, Rhode Island. He was the son of Huguenots Hiram and Emeline Ballou.

He studied at Brown University and the National Law School located in Ballston, NY. He was admitted to the Rhode Island bar in 1853. Sullivan was married to Sarah Hart Shumway on October 15, 1855, and they had two sons, Edgar and Willie. He served in the Rhode Island House of Representatives and ardently supported President Abraham Lincoln.

Sullivan answered the call by President Lincoln to amass 75,000 militia troops after the bombing of Fort Sumpter. Sullivan quickly volunteered and became a major in the Union Army. He would command the 2nd Rhode Island and fight at the First Battle of Bull Run.

Sullivan composed a letter to his wife on July 14, 1861. I include the letter in this book because it demonstrates his ability to convey his intimate feelings to his wife. This is something that I believe most husbands could improve upon. My wife and I visited his grave site, located in Swan Point Cemetery, Providence, Rhode Island in September 2021.

****

Headquarters, Camp Clark
Washington, D.C.
July 14, 1861
My very dear Sarah:

The indications are very strong that we shall move in a few days – perhaps tomorrow. Lest I should not be able to write you again, I feel impelled to write lines that may fall under your eye when I shall be no more.

Our movement may be one of a few days duration and full of pleasure – and it may be one of sever conflict and death to me. Not my will, but thine O God, be done. If it is necessary that I should fall on the battlefield for my country, I am ready. I have no misgivings about, or lack of confidence in, the cause in which I am engaged, and my courage does not halt or falter. I know how strongly American Civilization now leans upon the triumph of the Government, and how great a debt we owe to those who went before us through the blood and suffering of the Revolution. And I am willing – perfectly willing – to lay down all my joys in this life, to help maintain this Government, and to pay that debt.

But, my dear wife, when I know that with my own joys I lay down nearly all of yours, and replace them in this life with cares and sorrows – when, after having eaten for long years the bitter fruit of orphanage myself, I must offer it as their only sustenance to my dear little children – is it weak or dishonorable, while the banner of my purpose floats calmly and proudly in the breeze, that my unbounded love for you, my darling wife and children, should struggle in fierce, though useless, contest with my love of country.

Sarah, my love for you is deathless, it seems to bind me to you with mighty cables that nothing buy Omnipotence could break; and yet my love of Country comes over me like a strong wind and bears me irresistibly on with all these chains to the battlefield.

The memories of the blissful moments I have spent with you come creeping over me, and I feel most gratified to God and to you that I have enjoyed them so long. And hard it is for me to given them up and burn to ashes the hopes of futures years, when God willing, we might still have lived and loved together and seen our sons grow up to honorable manhood around us. I have, I know, but few and small claims upon Divine Providence, but something whispers to me – perhaps it is the wafted prayer of my little Edgar – that I shall return to my loved ones unharmed, If I do not, my dear Sarah, never forget how much I love you, and when my last breath escapes me on the battlefield, it will whisper your name.

Forgive my many faults, and the many pains I have caused you. How thoughtless and foolish I have often been! How gladly would I wash out with my tears every little spot upon your happiness, and struggle with all the misfortune of this world, to shield you and my children from harm. But I cannot. I must watch you from the spirit land and hover near you, while you buffet the storms with your precious little freight, and wait with sad patience till we meet to part no more.

But, O Sarah! If the dead can come back to this earth and flit unseen around those they loved, I shall always be near you; in the brightest days and in the darkest night –amidst your happiest scenes and gloomiest hours – always, always; and if the be a soft breeze upon your cheek, it shall be my breath, or the cool air fans your throbbing temple, it shall be my spirit passing by.

Sarah, do not mourn me dead; think I am gone and wait for me, for we shall meet again.

As for my little boys, they will grow as I have done, and never know a father's love and care. Little Willie is too young to remember me long, and my blue-eyed Edgar will keep my frolics with him among the dimmest memories of his childhood. Sarah, I have unlimited confidence in your maternal care and your development of their characters.

Tell my two mothers his and hers I call God's blessing upon them.

O Sarah, I wait for you there!!! Come to me and lead thither my children.

Sullivan

****

Major Sullivan Ballou was directing his troops while on horseback at the First Battle of Bull Run. He was hit by a six-pound Confederate cannon-ball. A portion of his right leg was dismembered and the remainder of the leg was amputated. Ballou died a week later.

He had written his letter to Sarah fifteen days before his death. It seems like he had a premonition that he would perish at the Battle of Bull Run. His letter is a challenge to us as men to let our wives know how much they mean to us.

[The historical notes concerning Sullivan Ballou were derived from Wikipedia.

The letter written by Sullivan Ballou was derived from <u>www.nps.gov/resources</u>]

Many things can prove to be deterrents to improving the intimacy side of the Triangle

of Marriage. Consider the following...

Complacency – taking each other for granted. Being self-satisfied and not couple focused.

Cantankerous – Does anyone enjoy being around a person who is continually argumentative? Do you?

Curmudgeon – exhibiting a bad temper...I really hate discussing this one.

Controlling – demonstrating a 'my way or the highway' attitude.

Cynical – having a cynical attitude projects a lack of trust and sincerity.

Chameleon – just wanting to blend in and not offer your opinion. Emotional camouflage is their favorite fashion.

Condescending – I would take time to explain, but I doubt you'd understand.

Capriciousness – dominated by impulsiveness and unpredictability.

Clairvoyance – demonstrating an assurance in reading the mind of your spouse. Reading minds is not an exact science and probably not worth the risk.

Cataract Vision – the glass is always half empty. The power of optimistic thinking must be considered detrimental.

Cryptic – communicating in vague and hidden agenda messages.

Critical – persistently expressing judgmental characterizations of behavior.

Commonsense – inability to connect the dots concerning the sowing and reaping principle. Commonsense, like Elvis, has seemingly left the building and unfortunately some marriages. On a side note, commonsense needs a revival in the United States.

Character – lack of integrity in various aspects of life creates illusions of morality.

Cognizance – being aware and intentional in meeting the needs of our spouse. If your bride changes her hair color – you should probably notice and carefully acknowledge.

Civility – conducting yourself in a manner that proves you respect your spouse. Lack of civility is demeaning.

Contrite – if you never admit you're wrong – you're wrong.

Commanding – if you treat your wife as an enlistee or employee – you are inviting trouble.

Childlikeness – your wife did not marry you to raise you.

Credit – be careful to give credit where credit is due...and don't take credit when it's not yours.

Consolation – be willing to demonstrate empathy in times of disappointment or loss.

Be compassionate.

Consideration – try your very best to not be deliberately hurtful to your spouse.

Collaborate – unilateral decision-making will not be a way to help your spouse to have healthy self-esteem.

Contention – better to be a peacemaker than a provoker.

Contentment – continually convey satisfaction in your marriage. Also, one thing the Amish have right – simplicity in life is a good thing.

The wisest counsel to offer that will improve intimacy was stated by the greatest teacher in history:

"So, whatever you wish that others would do to you, do also to them, for this is the Law and the Prophets."
[Matthew 7:12 – ESV]

My wife and I enjoy visiting the Lancaster, PA area. It is fascinating to observe the simple ways of the Amish folks. Our favorite restaurant is the 'Good 'N Plenty' where you are served family style and often have the opportunity to dialogue with other visitors. The food is good and there is plenty of it!!! While visiting the Lancaster area we make it a priority to watch one of the excellent plays at the Sight and Sound Theatre. We have really appreciated the Biblically related productions of 'Moses', 'Abraham', 'The Miracle of Christmas', 'In the Beginning', 'Joseph', 'Jonah' and 'Esther'.

It is also enjoyable to just drive around the Lancaster area watching horse-drawn farming techniques being utilized by the Amish. One of the most common sights is the horse-drawn carriage. The towns in the immediate area have intriguing names:

Paradise, Ephrata, Lititz, Bird in Hand, Conestoga, and Blue Ball, etc. My favorite town name by far in Intercourse, Pennsylvania. For most men the word intercourse immediately arouses their sexual interest and desire. The village of Intercourse was formerly known as "Cross Keys". Cross Keys was an old tavern stand that stood at what is now known as Intercourse. The Old King's highway that connected Philadelphia and Pittsburgh ran east-west through here. And the roadway between Wilmington and Erie crossed north-south at this location. The tavern was a place to talk and communicate. It was a place to exchange opinions, fellowship, enjoy a meal together and catch up on information. These types of communication need to be evident in the intimacy side of the marriage.

I looked up the definition of the word intercourse in the Oxford Language Dictionary and the primarily stated meaning is: "communication or dealings between individuals or groups". This definition is followed by: 'short for sexual intercourse'.

Most husbands who come with their wives for marital counseling have a preconceived notion that intercourse is only sexual in nature. I carefully distinguish that there is a distinction between intimacy and passion. Intimacy refers to the communication that must be present in the marriage that proves that your spouse is significant and secure in the marriage. Passion is the sexual part of the marriage triangle that will be discussed in the final section of this book. If the couple is experiencing difficulties in the intimacy side of their marriage, they automatically experience frustrations in the passionate side of their marriage.

Mayberry, RFD...just an observation...
Andy Taylor – Sheriff - widowed
Barney Fife – Deputy Sheriff - not married
Aunt Bee Taylor – widowed
Thelma Lou – Teacher - single and dating Andy
Goober Pyle – Auto Mechanic - not married
Gomer Pyle – not married
Floyd – Barber – not married
Howard Sprague – County Clerk – not married
Otis Campbell – only character married and town drunk
who checked himself in and out of the jail!!!

Sharing laughs together is a terrific stress reducer for couples. Laughter is proven medically to strengthen your immune system, improve your overall mood, diminish the intensity of pain and reduce blood pressure. {Laughter is the Best Medicine – HelpGuide.org}

> *Laughter is a potent endorphin releaser.*

> *Laughter contagiously forms social bonds.*

> *Laughter fosters brain connectivity.*

> *Laughter is central to relationships.*

> *Laughter has an effect similar to antidepressants.*

> *Laughter protects your heart.*

> *{Six Science-Based Reasons Why Laughter Is*

The Best Medicine – David DiSalvo / Forbes -

June 5, 2017}

> *"A joyful heart is good medicine,*
> *but a broken spirit dries up*
> *the bones."*
> *[Proverbs 17:22 – NASB]*

Humor is medicinal to the soul and a therapeutic release to be shared by couples.

Red Skelton's Recipe For The Perfect Marriage

1. *Two times a week we go to a nice restaurant, have a little beverage, good food and companionship. She goes Tuesdays, I go on Fridays.*

2. *We also sleep in separate beds. Hers is in California and mine is in Texas.*

3. *I take my wife everywhere, but she keeps finding her way back.*

4. *I asked my wife where she wanted to go for our anniversary. "Somewhere I haven't been in a long time!" she said. So I suggested the kitchen.*

5. *We always hold hands. if I let go, she shops.*

6. *My wife told me the car wasn't running well because there was water in the carburetor. I asked where the car was. She told me, "In the lake".*

7. *She got a mud pack and looked great for two days. Then the mud fell off.*

8. *She ran after the garbage truck, yelling, "Am I too late for the garbage?" The driver said, "No, jump in!"*

9. *Remember: Marriage is the number one cause of divorce.*

10. *I married Miss Right. I just didn't know her first name was 'Always'.*

The verbal and physical affirmations of our love for each other improves the level of intimacy and leads to commitment. Couples prove that they are significant to each other and secure in their relationship. They trust each other and it is then appropriate to enter the Covenant of Marriage. An unwavering commitment to continue to honor the Covenant of Marriage is essential for an enduring commitment.

It becomes problematic if the couple has not invested enough time together to bond their relationship to a high level of intimacy. After intimacy has been demonstrated and the couple enters the Covenant of Marriage; they can then enjoy the passionate part of their relationship without guilt. Becoming passionately involved prior to developing a high level of intimacy and entering the Covenant of Marriage, is detrimental to longevity.

The intimacy or cleaving dimension of the marriage speaks directly to the need to bond the relationship emotionally. An indispensable ingredient in intimacy is companionship.

Companionship includes investing time with each other. Companionship involves being completely transparent and honest in your communication. Intimacy is a dynamic portion of the Covenant of Marriage that requires continual maintenance and growth for the marriage.

Cleaving to one another appropriately in the Covenant of Marriage will provide proof that the husband and wife are significant and secure with each other.

ONE FLESH – PASSION – EROS

> *"Therefore a man shall leave*
> *his father and his mother and*
> *hold fast to his wife, and they*
> *shall become one flesh.*
> *And the man and his wife*
> *were both naked and were*
> *both naked and were not ashamed.*
> *[Genesis 2:24,25 – ESV]*

ONE FLESH – PASSION – EROS

It is time to discuss the third and final component of the Triangle of Marriage.

That third component is the couple becoming 'one flesh' – which I will be referring to as the Passionate portion of the Triangle of Marriage.

> *Leave – Commitment – Agape*
> *Cleave – Intimacy – Phileo*
> *One flesh – Passion – Eros*

The passionate part of the marriage should be a celebration of the Covenant of Marriage. The passionate component of the marriage is the most physically pleasurable experience that God has created. The passionate part of the relationship is designed to be shared in the Safety, Sanctity, and Security of the Covenant of Marriage. This is summarized in Genesis 2:25 as the couple becoming 'one flesh' and 'both were naked and not ashamed'.

A disturbing trend over the last five decades is the increase of nudity and sexual promiscuity portrayed on television and in movies. These actors are performing in various stages of nudity and there is no shame. Passion is being trivialized and modesty is being mocked. Sexual immorality is being depicted as the norm. Actors and actresses depict fornication and adultery without any moral foundation or compass.

"I mow my yard".
One day shortly after joining the PGA
Tour in 1965, Lee Trevino, a professional
golfer and married man, was at his home
in Dallas, Texas, mowing his front yard,
as he always did. A lady driving by in a big,
shiny Cadillac stopped in front of his home,
lowered the window and asked, "Excuse me,
do you speak English?" Lee responded, 'Yes
Ma'am, I do'. The lady then asks, "What do
you charge to do yard work?"
Lee said, "Well, the lady in this house lets me
sleep with her." The lady hurriedly put the car
into gear and sped off!!!
[StanzStories.com]

My first Sociology Professor at Fairmont State College in the spring semester of 1969 made a prediction that has become increasingly true. He indicated that by the end of the century sex would be as common as a handshake. The general moral condition on most college campuses, beginning in the late 1960s, was 'if it feels good do it'. The sexual revolution began, and our society has continued down a path of moral decadence.

*Fred and Wilma Flintstone
were the first TV couple to
sleep in the same bed!!
[1960-1966
And they were married!!!
"Yabba, Dabba, Do"!!!
The first live actors to be
shown in bed together were
Herman and Lilly Munster.
{1964-1966*

*The first live actors, who
were not 'monsters', to be
shown in bed together were
Bob Newhart and Suzanne
Pleshette in 1974
[TV Guide]*

Sensuality and sexuality permeate television programming, the movie industry and the music industry. Young people are being subjected to sexual content and issues way too early in their lives.

Donald Duck comics were banned from Finland

because he doesn't wear trousers.
[SouthFloridaReporter.com
May 4, 2018]

Desmond John Morris was an English author who studied and authored books in human sociobiology. He authored the "Naked Ape" and conducted extensive studies in human pair bonding {Wikipedia}. I want to present an overview of the Twelve Steps of Pair Bonding.

These steps generally mirror the Leave, Cleave, and One-flesh principles outlined in the scriptures. These twelve pair bonding steps are essential in the sequential development of relationships as they develop over a period of time. Some of the initial steps can occur in rapid succession.

Twelve Steps of Pair Bonding – Desmond Morris

1. *Eye to Body*
2. *Eye to Eye*
3. *Voice to Voice*
4. *Hand to Hand*
5. *Arm to Shoulder*
6. *Arm to Waist*
7. *Face to Face*
8. *Hand to Head*
9. *Hand to Body*
10. *Mouth to Breast*
11. *Hand to Genital*
12. *Genital to Genital*
[MYEDATE.COM]

Eye to Body

What attracted you to your spouse? Men and women are attracted to each other in a variety of ways. A good friend of mine was attracted to his wife because he found her neck to be particularly attractive. I was initially attracted to my bride due to her gams – great legs!!!

I would submit that most relationships are initiated because we like what we see. The scriptures provide us with some examples of people who possess good looks.

Rachel
"…but Rachel was beautiful in form
and appearance". Rachel was a knock-out
in the eyes of Jacob!
[Genesis 29:17]

Joseph
"Now Joseph was handsome in form
and appearance".
[Genesis 39:6]

Queen Vashti –
Queen of Persia. King Ahasuerus commanded her
to come to his party with the guys "in order to show the peoples and
the princes her beauty, for she was lovely to look at".
[Esther 1:11 – ESV]

Esther
"The young woman had a beautiful figure and was
lovely to look at".
[Ester 2:7 – ESV]

The 'Eye to Body' step is the discovery of a person of interest. It is a pleasurable observation where the mind makes a positive assessment. It is kind of an 'eureka' moment.

Each person possesses an innate set of criteria that is automatically engaged when we make visual observations. It is one thing to appreciate beauty and be drawn to the person; it is not appropriate for this initial observation to be lustful in nature.

> *"I made a covenant with*
> *my eyes not to look*
> *lustfully at a young*
> *woman..."*
> *[Job 31:1 – NIV]*

Joseph was sold into slavery by his brothers. He was purchased by Potiphar and worked in the home of this influential Egyptian. The scripture records that Potiphar's wife 'cast her eyes on Joseph and said, "Lie with me." Mrs. Potiphar was obviously attracted to Joseph but was only interested in a passionate, sexual experience. She was only interested in committing adultery and enjoying the passionate pleasure. Joseph resisted her advances and was falsely accused of sexual harassment. Joseph was imprisoned because of these false accusations. God would remain faithful to Joseph and eventually would elevate him to the position of V.P. – Vice Pharoah. This event took place approximately 3,800 years ago and is one of the earliest recorded incidents of sexual harassment.

> *"Well Friday 'bout a week ago*
> *Leroy shootin' dice*
> *And at the edge of the bar*
> *Sat a girl named Doris*
> *And oh that girl looked nice*

When he cast his eyes upon her
And the trouble soon began
And Leroy Brown had learned a lesson
"Bout a-messin' with the wife of
A jealous man"
[Bad, Bad, Leroy Brown by
Jim Croce – 1973]
[Beware of your motives
when making Eye-to-Body
observations.]

Herod Antipas, or King Herod the Tetrarch, provides us with an example of how to use the eye-to-body evaluation inappropriately. He was the son of King Herod the Great and ruled the province of Galilee during the time of YESHUA. YESHUA contemptuously referred to Herod the Tetrarch as 'that fox'. [Luke 13:32 – ESV] Herod the Tetrarch divorced his first wife who was the Nabataean daughter of Aretas IV. Herod subsequently married Herodias who had previously been married to his half-brother. This marriage caused a significant amount of turmoil in Israel. John the Baptist confronted Herod by saying: "It is not lawful for you to have your brother's wife." [Mark 6:18 - ESV]

Herodias was greatly offended when John the Baptist confronted her husband. She desired to have John the Baptist executed, but the scriptures inform us that "Herod feared John, knowing that he was a righteous and holy man, and kept him safe." [Mark 6:20 – ESV]

Herod hosted a birthday party and the daughter of Herodias, Salome, performed a dance. The dance was so pleasing to Herod that he told Herodias he would grant her a wish, even up to half of his kingdom. She then asked for the head of John the Baptist. John was martyred by being beheaded. It appears that Salome had danced seductively, and Herod's eyes were viewing her body inappropriately. His lust enabled him to commit murder.

King David fell into a similar temptation. King David was supposed to be on the battlefield commanding the army as they fought against the Ammonites. Instead, he was in his palace on the rooftop overlooking the village of Silwan in what is now referred to as the City of David. He cast his view across the valley and observed Bathsheba bathing. The scripture describes Bathsheba as being 'very beautiful'. King David was pleased with his eye-to-body observation. King David lusted after Bathsheba and committed adultery which resulted in pregnancy. King David eventually became involved in a plot that resulted in the murder of Uriah, the Hittite, the husband of Bathsheba. I have stood at the very location of King David's palace, and you can easily understand how King David could have viewed Bathsheba. His initial eye-to-body observation caused him to succumb to temptation. It took King David about a year to repent and be restored in his relationship with YHWH. Take a moment to read II Samuel 11 which describes in detail the account of King David and Bathsheba. You can also read and study about the remorse and repentance of King David in Psalm 51. Thankfully, we serve GOD, who is slow to anger, abundant in lovingkindness, and desires to forgive…Jonah 4:2. King David was restored to GOD. Dr. Luke offers this assessment of King David: "I have found in David the son of Jesse a man after my heart, who will do all my will." [Acts 13:22 –ESV] King David was not perfect, but he was perfectly forgiven. We can experience the same forgiveness in our lives by placing our faith in YESHUA. After King David experienced forgiveness and restoration, Dr. Luke, in Acts 13:36 [ESV], indicates that he 'served the purpose of God in his own generation." May the same be true of us.

"I thought love was only
true in fairy tales

Meant for someone else,
but not for me.
Love was out to get me
That's the way it seemed
Disappointment haunted
all my dreams

Then I saw her face, now
I'm a believer
Not a trace of doubt in
my mind
I'm in love, I'm a believer
I couldn't leave her if I tried."
['I'm A Believer' –
The Monkees – 1966]

This song emphasizes the power of an initial glance and subsequent observation. I don't believe in 'love at first sight', but I do believe in 'interest at first sight'.

It is vital to guard our eyes and to make appropriate assessments of who we observe.

The initial observations we make of this person of interest are likely private in nature.

Once we have processed enough of what we have seen, we make the determination that this person is worth a prolonged or second look. It is at this juncture that the second step of pair bonding will take place.

The following information was obtained from REGAIN.US in an article posted 08/03/2021: "What Makes A Guy Attractive? Physical and

Personality Traits." These results are based on studies they completed concerning what women find attractive in men.

I am inserting these now for consideration as you ponder the Twelve Steps of Pair Bonding.

See how many of these characteristics can be ascertained with an "Eye-to-Body" observation.

Assess where the other characteristics are assessed in the development of Pair Bonding.

- ➤ *Facial Hair & Body Hair*
  - ○ *They postulate that this lends to a look of maturity.*
  - ○ *Samson and John the Baptist would probably fare well in this characteristic*
  - ○ *A little chest hair seems to be fine...a jungle is unacceptable.*
  - ○ *How would Esau fare in this assessment? When he was born, he was a hairy little guy! [Genesis 25:25] This characteristic continued and was used by Rebekah to trick Isaac into blessing Jacob. [Genesis 27]*
- ➤ *Sincerity*
  - ○ *The demonstration of a desire to get to know the woman.*
  - ○ *In this day of casual sex and reduced interest in commitment, sincerity is lacking.*
- ➤ *Ability to Tell a Good Story*
  - ○ *This would be indicative of a high level of communication.*
  - ○ *The ability to communicate, as indicated previously, is essential in developing the intimacy component of the relationship.*
- ➤ *Signs of Physical Activity*
  - ○ *Women appear to be attracted to muscle development – biceps and legs.*

- o *According to one of the guides at Colonial Williamsburg, the term "put your best foot forward" referred to a gentleman showing off his calf muscle – which was indicative that he was a good equestrian.*
- ➤ *Sense of Humor*
  - o *Able to tell a joke and make her laugh*
  - o *"A joyful heart is good medicine..." – Proverbs 17:22 – ESV*
- ➤ *Being Into Music*
  - o *A diversity of musical interests seems to be an attractive quality*
  - o *I heard this 'through the grapevine'.*
- ➤ *Intelligence*
  - o *Able to converse effectively*
  - o *Having a random fund of trivial information makes for interesting conversation.*
  - o *Comparable intellectual levels promote pair bonding.*
- ➤ *Smelling Good*
  - o *Natural scent is important.*
  - o *Enhanced scent with cologne...make sure she likes it*
  - o *Women remember the scent of a man [and vice versa]*
  - o *Our olfactory sense is the sense most closely associated with memory*
- ➤ *Good Hair*
  - o *Women are more attracted to a full head of hair.*
  - o *Guys without hair are gaining though!!*
  - o *Is this why Rogaine is so popular??*
- ➤ *Volunteering*
  - o *Demonstrating a compassionate heart*
  - o *Having a concept of the 'greater good'*
- ➤ *Showing Passion*
  - o *Demonstrates a level of seriousness and commitment*
  - o *Be involved in something specific.*
- ➤ *Work Ethic*

- o *Demonstration of being able to pull your own weight*
- o *Can provide for her as needed*
- o *Evidence that you do not squander time*
- o *The overall work ethic in the USA today is deteriorating*
- ➢ *Having Confidence*
  - o *Study shows that women do not prefer shyness*
  - o *Women prefer decisiveness.*
  - o *Not prideful or boastful*
- ➢ *Being a Gentleman*
  - o *Manners have not gone out of style*
  - o *Be courteous in speech and behavior.*
- ➢ *Integrity*
  - o *Being honest and respectful is still in vogue and attractive*
  - o *Just tell the truth.*
- ➢ *Dominance*
  - o *This is in terms of being masculine. Masculinity has come under attack in our country in recent years.*
  - o *Taking the lead when appropriate*
  - o *Being decisive*
  - o *This is not male chauvinism.*
  - o *Promote a sense of safety and security*

*The men in the Bodi Tribe of Ethiopia are
considered more alluring to their women if
they possess 'bigger bellies'.
The Bodi men participate in what is called
the "Ka'el" Ceremony. The ceremony consists
of entrants selected by their family clan. It is
actually a competition to determine which man
is the most obese. The men will isolate and
consume a concoction of cows blood and milk
to produce more belly fat.*

[Operanewsapp.com – 08/20/2021]
Hmmmmm!!!!

Guys are visually oriented. Here are some of the primary characteristics that men look for when making 'Eye-to-Body' assessments.

- *Legs*
- *Eyes*
- *Breasts*
- *Lips*
- *Clean skin*
- *Butt*
- *Hair*
- *Figure*
- *Smile*
- *Grooming*

According to the American Society of Plastic Surgeons, Americans spent more than $16.5 billion on cosmetic surgery in 2018!! The types of surgeries most popular are listed below:

- *Breast augmentation – 313,735 procedures*
- *Liposuction – 258,558 procedures*
- *Eyelid surgery – 206,529 procedures*
- *Labiaplasty – 10,246 procedures*
- *Facelift – 121, 531 procedures*
- *Tummy tuck – 130,081 procedures*
- *Breast reduction – 43,591 procedures*
- *Nose reshaping – 213,780 procedures*

Catherine Elizabeth Middleton [Kate] married Prince William, Duke of Cambridge on April 29, 2011. It was one of the most viewed marriage ceremonies in history. Kate's sister, Pippa, created quite a stir with the dress who wore to the wedding which accentuated her butt.

There was an increase in the plastic surgery business for women to have their butt shaped to match Pippa's! [SMH!!!] What does the Bible have to say about beauty?

> *"Charm is deceitful,*
> *and beauty is vain,*
> *but a woman who fears*
> *the LORD is to be*
> *praised.*
> *Give her the fruit of her*
> *hands, and let her works*
> *praise her in the gates."*
> *[Proverbs 31:30, 31 – ESV]*

An article printed in 'scienceofpeople.com' takes us on a tour of the evolution of beauty and body types.

"Beauty Standards: See How Body Types Change Through History"

- ➢ *Ancient Egypt [c. 1292-1069 B.C.]*
  - o *Slender*
  - o *Narrow Shoulders*
  - o *High Waist*
  - o *Symmetrical Face*
  - o *I.e. – Queen Nefertiti*
- ➢ *Ancient Greece [c. 500-300 B.C.]*
  - o *Plump*
  - o *Full-bodied*
  - o *Light Skin*
  - o *I.e. – sculptures of Aphrodite*

➢ *Han Dynasty [c. 206 B.C. – 220 A.D.]*
  o *Slim Waist*
  o *Pale Skin*
  o *Large Eyes*
  o *Small Feet*
  o *Long black hair, white teeth and red lips*
  o *I.e. – Wang Zhaojun*
➢ *Italian Renaissance [c. 1400-1700]*
  o *Ample Bosom*
  o *Rounded Stomach*
  o *Full Hips*
  o *Fair Skin*
  o *I.e. – Simonetta Cattaneo*
➢ *Victorian England [c. 1837-1901]*
  o *Desirably Plump*
  o *Full-figured*
  o *Cinched-waist [era of the popularization of the corset]*
  o *I.e.. – Queen Victoria, "Gibson" Girl [1890's]*
➢ *Roaring Twenties [c. 1920's]*
  o *Flat Chest*
  o *Downplayed Waist*
  o *Shor Bob Hairstyle*
  o *Boyish Figure*
  o *Androgynous Look*
  o *I.e. – Marie Claire*
➢ *Golden Age of Hollywood [c. 1930's-1950's]*
  o *Curves*
  o *Hourglass Figure*
  o *Large Breasts*
  o *Slim Waist*
  o *I.e. – Marilyn Monroe, Elizabeth Taylor*
➢ *Swinging Sixties [c. 1960s]*
  o *Willowy*

- *Thin*
- *Long, slim Legs*
- *Adolescent Physique*
- *I.e. – Twiggy*
- *Supermodel Era [c.1980s]*
  - *Athletic*
  - *Svelte, but Curvy*
  - *Tall*
  - *Toned Arms*
  - *I.e.. – Cindy Crawford*
  - *This era saw an increase in exercise involvement. Also saw an increase in anorexia.*
- *Heroine Chic [c. 1990s]*
  - *Waifish*
  - *Extremely Thin*
  - *Translucent Skin*
  - *Androgynous*
  - *Ie. – Kate Moss*
- *Postmodern Beauty [c. 2000s – today]*
  - *Flat Stomach*
  - *'Healthy' Skinny*
  - *Large Breasts + Butt*
  - *Thigh Gap*
  - *I.e.. – Gisele Bundchen*

Actor Pierce Brosnan, James Bond actor, and his wife Keely Shaye Smith were married in 2000. When they were celebrating their 20th Anniversary, some folks pointed out that she had gained a significant amount of weight over the last twenty years. Brosnan replied: "She is in my eyes the most beautiful woman in the world, she raised my five children with love, in the past, I already loved her for her personality and not just for her beauty. Now I love her even more. I am very proud of her, and I always try to be worth of her love."

[Credit: Marie Claire Dorking, Yahoo!Life / 09/29/2021]

Relationships that do not develop beyond the physical attraction are likely doomed to fail. We all change in our physical appearance over time. I sometimes look in the mirror at a seventy-year-old man and ask: "Who is that?!" We may be initially attracted to physical characteristics, but for the relationship to mature and develop in a health manner, emotional bonding must become a reality. The emotional bonding is nurtured in the intimacy or cleaving part of the marriage.

"Charm is deceitful,
and beauty is vain,
but a woman who fears
the LORD is to be
praised.
Give her of the fruit
of her hands, and let
her works praise her
in the gates."
[King Lemuel – 3,000
years ago...
Proverbs 31:30,31}

Find someone who will love
your soul more than your body.
[1positivewomen / Instagram]

"'Cause I got a couple dents in
my fender
Got a couple rips in my jeans

Try to fit the pieces together
But perfection is my enemy
On my own I'm so clumsy
But on Your shoulders I can see
I'm free to be me
["Free To Be Me" by
Francesa Battestelli]

Eye to Eye

If you observe a person long enough, eye-to-eye contact will materialize. The 'object' of your attention looks back. Sometimes that can be a feeling of 'getting caught' or peering through a keyhole and there is an eye gazing back at you. You know when someone is looking at you and whether that is a look of awakened interest. When eye-to-eye occurs, messages are able to be instantaneously transmitted. If the person is also interested, then the look is more than just a passing glance. This non-verbal interaction can immediately convey mutual interest. It is even possible to transmit a 'flirting' message indicative of a positive connection.

The eyes can also immediately transmit a message of not being interested at all. A visual 'shut down' can eliminate any further progression of pair bonding.

"The eye is the lamp
of the body. So, if your
eye is healthy, your
whole body will be
full of light, but if your
eye is bad, your whole

*body will be full of
darkness."
[Message from YESHUA
Matthew 6:22,23 – ESV]*

*"Whoever winks his eyes
plans dishonest things;
he who purses his lips
brings evil to pass."
[Proverbs 16:30 – ESV]
[Be careful to read the
non-verbal eye messages
accurately!!!]*

Another way of phrasing this verse is: "The eye is the window to the soul." It is quite possible to gain understanding into a person's emotions by looking into their eyes. You can fake a smile, but it is difficult to fake the message that your eyes are conveying. The pupil is our light regulator. The pupil is a primary source of gathering information. Our vision becomes an essential sense in pair bonding. Over time a 'wink of the eye' can become a special method of communication between the sender and receiver. The message being transmitted is intended for a limited audience and in pair-bonding the 'audience' is two people.

Powerful messages, positive and negative, can be conveyed instantly via eye contact. When YESHUA was arrested He was brought before Caiaphas, the High Priest.

Peter was in the courtyard during this legal proceeding, and it was in this location that he would deny the LORD three times. Immediately after the third denial the rooster crowed just as the LORD had previously revealed Peter. It was at that very moment that Peter and Jesus made eye contact.

This scene was powerfully portrayed in the 2004 movie, "The Passion of the Christ" produced by Mel Gibson.

> *"And the LORD turned and*
> *looked at Peter. And Peter*
> *remembered the saying of*
> *the LORD, how HE said to*
> *him, "Before the rooster*
> *crows today, you will deny*
> *me three times." And he*
> *went out and wept bitterly."*
> *{Luke 22:61,62}*

We know the rest of the story as Peter and JESUS reconciled on the shores of the Sea of Galilee. The 'look' that Jesus gave to Peter was a look of confirmation concerning the truth HE had told Peter previously. It was not a look of condemnation. It was a look of concern and caring that would eventually allow them to reconnect.

> *"Something in your eyes*
> *Was so inviting*
> *Something in your smile*
> *Was so exciting..."*

['Strangers in the Night' –
Frank Sinatra – 2010]

We possess the capability of sending and receiving powerful messages by making eye contact. If in a split second, or prolonged eye-to-eye contact, a smile ensues – the third step in pair bonding can be realized.

Voice to Voice

This stage of pair bonding allows the couple to engage in incidental conversation.

Where are you from? What kind of work do you do? Initial assessments are being conducted concerning interests and activities. Do you like the accent of the person? What does the verbal interaction tell you about the intellectual abilities of the person? Is the person introverted or extroverted? Is this person only interested in talking about themselves? Is there a real communication transpiring?

> *"There are doubtless many different languages in the world, and none is without meaning, but if I do not know the meaning of the language, I will be a foreigner to the speaker and the speakers a foreigner to me."*
> *[I Corinthians 14:10,11 – ESV]*

Direct and indirect messages are conveyed by voice inflection and tone. Complimentary words and engaging in meaningful dialogue will bolster the possibility of setting up a formal meeting or date. If the verbal interaction proves to be positive, then names and cell numbers will be exchanged. There is intention by both parties to meet again in person.

"And her voice
It's sweet as angels sighing

And her voice
It's warm as summer sky
And that sound
It haunts my dreams
And spins me 'round
Until it seems
I'm flying..."
{"Her Voice"
Prince Eric to Little Mermaid
Sung by Graham Phillips}

When a couple communicates voice-to-voice, it is critical to use our words wisely. The Apostle Paul accentuated this in his letter to the church at Colossae.

"Let your speech always
be gracious, seasoned with
salt, so that you may know
how you ought to answer
each person."
[Colossians 4:6 – ESV]

Why do we use salt? To season our food and make it more palatable. Gracious and kind speech even from the very onset of communication will communicate volumes about us to the other person. Genuinely gracious and kind words assist in 'stacking the deck' in favor of additional contacts and progress in the pair bonding process. An emotional interest may begin at this phase of pair bonding, but not at the level of an emotional connection.

Hand to Hand

When the next in person meeting [date] occurs, the couple will make additional eye-to-body observations and eye-to-eye contact. Voice-to-voice conversation ensues and if positive vibes are conveyed, the couple takes the next step in pair-bonding of holding hands. This is not necessarily occurring on the first date. In fact, several voice-to-voice meetings may be engaged prior to a hand-to-hand involvement.

*"And when I touch you
I feel happy inside
It's such a feelin' that my love
I can't hide
I can't hide
I can't hide*

*Yeah, you got that somethin'
I think you'll understand
When I feel that somethin'
I want to hold your hand
I want to hold your hand
I want to hold your hand
I want to hold your hand*

*["I Want To Hold Your Hand"
The Beatles – 1964 – sold
over 1,000,000 records]*

The touching of hands is the next logical step in pair-bonding. The holding of hands is a Social Statement. We are with each other and interested in

each other. This is not shaking hands as in a greeting. This is a meaningful touch indicating some degree of mutual interest.

Holding of hands is a first step in physical affection. Holding hands is a skin-to-skin touch.

Touching feels good and can be indicative of a significant increase of interest in the person.

Our sense of touch enables us to experience a variety of sensations. We can detect degrees of temperature extremes such as heat or cold. Touch will notify us of pain. Touch also enables us to experience pleasure and develop intimacy. There is a principle that I believe is operational in relationships: "The more skin you touch, the more skin you want to touch." It is critical, in the appropriate development of intimacy, to keep the touch of skin to a healthy level. Touch connects us to our environment and touch can connect us to the other person in a very meaningful way.

Are you comfortable in your own skin?
[14ᵗʰ Century Old English metaphor]

"Thin- skinned" – too touchy, too sensitive.
[Old Oxford English – 1680]

"Thick-skinned" – over time became
a characteristic of one being insensitive
to criticism.
[1500s – Old Oxford English]

"Under One's Skin" – to irritate
someone intensely.

"Skin in the Game" – to have a
stake in something.
When a couple hold hands they
are messaging the other person that
they have 'Skin in the Game'.

[mentalfloss.com]

Meaningful and appropriate touch is essential to our development as human beings. A new-born infant that is immediately touched and held by their parents will feel significant and secure. Powerful messages are conveyed by touch. YESHUA used meaningful touch to demonstrate care, convey blessings, and transmit healing. The largest organ in the human body is the skin. Skin covers roughly two square meters of the body. Skin is a major source of obtaining information about our environment and the development of relationships.

How we hold hands and touch one another will provide additional information that will affect our opinions of each other. The sensation of touching hand-to-hand releases positive chemicals in our brain that are pleasure oriented. The initial handholding is still at a distance, like when you're seated beside each other at a movie or taking a walk together.

"Basic warm touch calms
cardiovascular stress. It activates
the body's vagus nerve, which is
intimately involved with our
compassionate response, and a
simple touch can trigger release of
oxytocin, aka 'the love hormone'.
[Hands of Research: The Science

of Touch / 09/29/2010]

"Your love is fading, I can feel
your love fading
Girl, it's fading away from me
'Cause your touch, your touch
has grown cold
As if someone else controls your
very soul
I've fooled myself long as I can
I can feel the presence of another man.

["I'm Losing You" -
The Temptations / 1966]

I enjoy watching an elderly couple taking a walk and still holding hands. I've seen couples who are well into their eighties and nineties holding hands. It's likely the way the physical bonding of their relationship began. Holding hands should never become passe.

Holding hands is one way to continue to demonstrate how much you care for your spouse.

Holding hands can stimulate a mental 'flashback' to the early days of your relationship.

Holding hands serves as a subtle, caring reminder of your significance to one another.

We need to be very aware of the power of touch. Many couples make the mistake of too much touching way too early in their relationship. Physical bonding begins with the hand-to-hand connection. Once the couple has progressed to physically touching, they begin connecting emotionally. Voice-to-voice interaction might include statements of "I like you".

"Where it began
I can't begin to know when
But then I know it's growing strong
Was in the spring
And spring became the summer
Who'd have believed you'd come along

Hands, touchin' hands
Reachin out, touchin' me, touchin' you

['Sweet Caroline' - Neil Diamond – 1969]

Arm To Shoulder

As physical interaction continues to increase, we then move beyond the hand-to-hand stage of pair bonding. The next sequential step is arm-to-shoulder. This is a step in the pair bonding process that is drawing the couple more and more towards each other. You can't be far apart when placing your hand on the shoulder of your person of interest. This is a possessive type of signaling in a positive sense of the word. It imparts a desire to become even closer in the relationship. This is an intentional and deliberate step to draw the person closer and increase the overall body-to-body contact. The arm-to-shoulder contact proves that the couple is becoming more comfortable with each other physically. It's a clear indication that the relationship is favorable and communicates a desire to continue to move forward intimately. At this point, the relationship remains at a casual level emotionally. It is a time of being carefree and just enjoying the company of the other person. It's at this point in the pair bonding process that we carve out even more time to spend together.

Arm To Waist

In the early phases of pair bonding, hand-to-hand and arm-to-shoulder contacts are typically done side-by-side. This is also true of the next phase in the pair bonding sequence which is arm-to-waist. When the relationship reaches the arm-to-waist phase, one typically observes a deepening of an emotional connection also. The couple is increasingly investing more time with one another. The level of their conversation becomes more engaging emotionally. Deeper discussions of opinions, likes, dislikes, and desires permeate their conversations. Arm-to-waist is more prolonged and demonstrates and even higher level of compatibility with one another. The couple is sharing more personal information and begins expressing their level of emotional connection. The couple becomes more private in their interaction, but can remain comfortable with public displays of affection. It is quite apparent that the couple is attracted to each other in a romantic sense. It becomes obvious to others that they are certainly more than just acquaintances or friends. Arm-to-waist is an external statement of physicality that demonstrates the level of intimacy is elevating.

Face To Face

After hand-to-hand, arm-to-shoulder and arm-to-waist phases have been experienced, the couple deepens their level of intimacy by turning face-to-face. They enjoy a frontal embrace and it's at this time the couple will share their first kiss.

"Does he love me, I wanna know
How can I tell if he loves me so?
Is it in his sighs?
Oh no, he'll make believe
If you wanna know
If he loves you so
It's in his kiss
That's where it is, oh yeah

In his warm embrace?
Oh no, that's just his arms
If you wanna know
If he loves you so
It's in his kiss
That's where it is...

["It's In His Kiss"
Cher – 1990]

Kissing is a major step in the development of intimacy. Kissing is a definite indication that the couple is deepening their romantic involvement. They are bonding together more closely from an intimacy perspective. It's

at this point that couples often make the decision to be exclusive with each other and make an agreement not to date anyone else.

Did you know that there is an "International Kissing Day?"
International Kissing Day is celebrated on July 6ᵗʰ annually.
What a great celebration!!!
Who knew??!!!

There are at least sixteen positive reasons for a couple to become involved in kissing at the appropriate level of pair bonding.

➢ *Kissing boosts your 'happy hormones'. Kissing triggers your brain to release a cocktail of chemicals that leave you feeling oh so good by igniting the pleasure centers of the brain. These chemicals include oxytocin, dopamine, and serotonin, which can make your feel euphoric and encourage feelings of affection and bonding.*

➢ *Kissing helps you bond with the other person. Oxytocin is a chemical that is released when you kiss and has been scientifically linked to pair bonding. Kissing causes an intensification of affection and improves the likelihood of attachment in pair bonding.*

➢ *Kissing has a tangible impact on your self-esteem. A person generally feels better about themselves if their partner is willing to engage in kissing activity.*

➢ *Kissing also relieves stress. And in my opinion, it is one of the very best stress reducers. We experience physiological benefits from kissing that assist us in our ability to manage stress.*

➢ *Kissing reduces anxiety. Kissing assists in calming us down. The oxytocin that is released in our brain when kissing increases our ability to relax and decreases anxiety levels.*

➢ *Kissing dilates your blood vessels, which helps reduce your blood pressure. Your heart rate increase while kissing and that dilates your blood vessels. This is according to Andrea Demirjian, who authored "Kissing: Everything You Ever Wanted to Know About One of Life's Sweetest Pleasures."*

➢ *Kissing can also assist in relieving cramps when a woman is enduring a painful period.*

➢ *Kissing can soothe headaches. The dilation of blood vessels which lowers our blood pressure can also be beneficial in the relief of headaches.*

➢ *Kissing can boost your immune system. Exchanging saliva exposes you to new germs that cause your body to boost the immune system.*

➢ *Kissing can reduce your response to allergies. Kissing has been proven to provide relief from hives and other types of allergic reactions. Stress tends to worsen reactions to allergens. As mentioned above, kissing increases our ability to handle stress and this can positively reduce the intensity of our allergic reactions.*

➢ *Kissing is linked to improvement in cholesterol levels. Results of a study conducted in 2009 found that couples who increase the frequency of kissing experienced an improvement of their total serum cholesterol.*

➢ *Kissing even helps prevent cavities by increasing saliva production. Kissing stimulates the salivary glands which increases the lubrication necessary for swallowing. This keeps food from adhering to our teeth thereby assisting in the prevention of tooth decay.*

➤ *Kissing is a solid barometer for physical compatibility with a romantic partner. Kissing is an essential component and activity that allows us to assess the suitability of a potential spouse. A survey of woman indicated that a first kiss can basically make or break it when it comes to attraction.*

➤ *Kissing romantically boosts your sex drive. As indicated in the initial part of this discussion on passion, the sexual part of the relationship is designed by our CREATOR to be expressed in the safety, security, and sanctity of the Covenant of Marriage.*

➤ *Kissing frequently helps you tighten and tone your facial muscles. We have thirty-four facial muscles and kissing can engage anywhere from two to thirty-four muscles.*

➤ *Kissing burns calories. A person is able to burn between two to twenty-six calories per minute depending on the passionate level of the kiss.*

[Credit to: "16 Reasons to Smooch: How Kissing Benefits Your Health by Adrienne Santos-Longhurst...posted on healthline. com...July 13, 2018]

Then He Kissed Me

"Well he walked up to me and he asked

me if I wanted to dance
He looked kinda nice and so I said
I might take a chance
When he danced he held me tight
And when he walked me home that night
All the stars were shining bright
And then he kissed me

Each time I saw him I couldn't wait to
see him again
I wanted to let him know that he was more
than a friend
I didn't know just what to do
So I whispered 'I love you'
And he said that he loved me too
And then he kissed me

He kissed me in a way that I've never
been kissed before
He kissed me in a way that I wanna be
Kissed forever more

I knew that he was mine so I gave him all
the love I had
And one day he took me home to meet his
mom and his dad
Then he asked me to be his bride
And always be right by his side
I felt so happy I almost cried
And then he kissed me."

[The Crystals – 1975]

[Kissing intensifies the physical and emotional connection and moves the relationship forward in pair bonding]

So, it is scientifically proven that kissing is healthy for us. And frankly it is an enjoyable activity!!!

Hand To Head

How many people do you let touch your head? Your barber or cosmetician, your dentist, reluctantly, or the optometrist are some who you allow to touch your head. We are very particular about who touches our head. Our head is perceived as an extremely vulnerable part of our body. A person must have achieved a high level of feeling significant, secure and safe to allow that special person to touch our head. Touching of the head reveals a 'high water mark' in terms of pair bonding. Touching and caressing the head is a trusting action that signals a removal of any defensiveness or questions of insecurity. The couple has proven the ability to trust one another, and trust is essential in the progression of pair bonding. Along with the physical affirmations experienced up to this point, the couple will continue to express their feelings to each other. Women, in general, are more adept at sharing on the emotional level. Men, in general, need to make more of an effort to express their feelings.

Hand To Body

The level of physicality intensifies and exploring and caressing more of the body ensues. Sexual stimulation is heightened and the couple must exercise high levels of caution.

The couple must be disciplined in order to not continue to the final phases of pair bonding prior to entering the Covenant of Marriage. Touching is limited by the couple continuing to be clothed during their physical exploration.

A couple who has progressed through the various stages of pair bonding will experience what I will refer to as a 'benchmark' progression. Once they have progressed to a certain stage, it is likely that stage will become the expectation for continuing the pair bonding process. They might rapidly experience all the prior stages, but it is difficult to revert to a previous stage and expect that earlier stage to become the norm. For example, once the couple has kissed, it's very difficult to stop kissing.

This study on pair bonding by Desmond Morris provides a scientifically surveyed and studied perspective on pair bonding. Each couple has decisions to personally make as to what is appropriate and how far to proceed at each step. As we consider the final three phases of pair bonding, Morris discovered that each culture studied had a ceremony, or ritual, that they expected the couple to enter prior to the consummation of the pair bonding process. I would submit that what Morris discovered in his study on pair bonding approximates the intentions of our Creator concerning Leaving, Cleaving, and becoming One Flesh as the couple heads toward the Covenant of Marriage.

In my opinion, a solid moral foundation is imperative to healthy pair bonding. The couple should prayerfully consider each step. The relationship is likely to endure if the couple progresses in pair bonding at a slow rate of speed. Entering the Covenant of Marriage prior to enjoying the final three steps of pair bonding will increase the likelihood of an enduring covenant. Many relationships are ruined when the couple progresses too quickly in pair bonding and engages in the final three phases prior to sealing their relationship with the Covenant of Marriage.

"..I found him whom my soul loves. I held him, and would not let him go.."
"I am my beloved's, and his desire is for me. Come, my beloved, Let us go out into the fields and lodge in the villages, let us go out early to the vineyards and see whether the vines have budded, whether the grape blossoms have opened and the pomegranates are in bloom. There I will give you my love. The mandrakes give forth Fragrance, and beside our doors are all choice fruits, new as well as old, which I have laid up for you, O my beloved."
[Song of Solomon 3:4 – ESV]

The Final Three Steps of Pair Bonding

Mouth To Breast

This is a uniquely human feature of passion. The husband feels, caresses and kisses the breast. The couple has retreated to complete privacy. The fondling of the breasts is a prelude to genital involvement.

> *"A bundle of myrrh [is] my*
> *well beloved unto me; he*
> *shall lie all night betwixt*
> *my breasts."*
> *[Song of Solomon 1:13*
> *KJV]*

> *"Your stature is like a palm*
> *tree and lay hold of its fruit.*
> *Oh may your breasts be like*
> *clusters of the vine, and the*
> *scent of your breath like*
> *apples."*
> *[Song of Solomon 7:8 –*
> *ESV]*

Hand To Genital

Gentle stimulation to elevate sensuality so that the final phase of passion can occur.

Genital To Genital

Face-to-face copulation is also uniquely human. Other positioning is possible, but it seems that most married couples would agree that the face-to-face approach is the most satisfying. Positional variety should be experimented to keep the passionate involvement interesting and fulfilling.

It is at this point in the relationship that the couple can realize the fulfillment of the first of the recorded 613 Laws of Torah...

> *"And GOD blessed them.*
> *And GOD said to them,*
> *"Be fruitful and multiply*
> *and fill the earth and subdue*
> *it...*
> *[Genesis 1:28 – ESV]*

Humans were created in the image of GOD. After the couple has completed this final phase of pair bonding, they can then bring another human being into existence.

Moses wrote an exclamatory comment after Adam and Eve became passionately involved...

> *"Therefore, a man shall leave*
> *His father and his mother and*
> *hold fast [cleave] to his wife,*
> *and they shall become*
> *one flesh [passion].*
> *And the man and his wife*
> *were both naked and were*

not ashamed.
[Genesis 2:24,25 – ESV]

The husband and wife have followed the direction and expectation of their Creator.

They have been involved in leaving, cleaving, and then sharing the passionate pleasure of being one flesh. They were 'not ashamed' as they have done things in accordance with the will of God. One problem in our country is that people are naked and not demonstrating any shame when they are using the sexual experience outside of the Covenant of Marriage.

Passion is designed by our Creator to be expressed and shared in the Safety, Security, and Sanctity of the Covenant of Marriage. Passion is the celebration of the Covenant of Marriage. In my opinion, passion is the most pleasurable physical experience designed by our Creator. Passion should be pleasurable for both the wife and the husband. Passion should be frequent enough that neither the husband or the wife should stray from the marriage covenant to engage in passion with any other person. Couples make huge mistakes in becoming involved in the passionate part of pair bonding before completing all the necessary physical and emotional phases of appropriate pair bonding.

"The husband should give
to his wife her conjugal rights,
and likewise, the wife to her
husband.
For the wife does not have
authority over her own body,
but the husband does. Likewise
the husband does not have
authority over his own body,
but the wife does.

Do not deprive one another,
except perhaps by agreement
for a limited time, that you may
devote yourselves to prayer,
but then come together again,
so that Satan may not tempt
you because of your lack of
self-control.
[I Corinthians 7:3-5 – ESV]

A major shift in the societal perspectives on passion [sex] in general has deteriorated rapidly since the 1960s. Fornication and adultery are portrayed in the media as the norm and in fact, condoned. This has led to a flippant and condescending view of passion and the Covenant of Marriage.

"Let marriage be held in
honor among all, and let
the marriage bed be undefiled,
for God will judge the
sexually immoral and
adulterous."
[Hebrews 13:4 – ESV]

The motto of the United States Marine Corp is "Semper Fidelis" which means 'always faithful". Being 'always faithful' to our spouse enables us to guard against one of the primary causes of divorce, which is adultery. This perspective is traditionally recited and exchanged in the marriage vows, 'forsaking all others'.

Sexual immorality was rampant in the city of Corinth in the first century. In fact, to 'Corinthianize' meant to commit 'sexual immorality'. Corinth was like modern day Las Vegas. Las Vegas makes a truckload of money on fulfillment of sexual fantasies. Located somewhere on the acro-Corinth was a temple dedicated to the worship of Aphrodite, the 'goddess of love'. According to the historian Strabo, prostitutes were engaged in sexually oriented 'religious services'. When the church was established in Corinth believers gathered on the Lord's Day to worship. But some of the guys were evidently still involved in the Wednesday service to 'worship' Aphrodite. Paul had a stern warning to the believers in Corinth.

> "The body is not meant
> for sexual immorality, but
> for the LORD, and the LORD
> for the body.
> And God raised the LORD
> and will also raise us up by
> HIS power. Do you not know
> that your bodies are members
> of Christ? Shall I then take
> the members of Christ and
> make them members of a prostitute?
> Never! Or do you not know that he
> who is joined to a prostitute
> becomes one body with her?
> For, as it is written, "The two
> will become one flesh."
> But he who is joined to the
> LORD, becomes one spirit
> with him.
> Flee from sexual immorality.
> Every other sin a person commits
> is outside the body, but the
> sexually immoral person sins against
> his own body."
> [I Corinthians 6:13-18]

Sin is sin. Sin has consequences. Sexual sin has consequences. Sexual sin permeates our society and culture. Unfortunately, sexual immorality is impacting the church at staggering levels. The enemy is alive and well and perpetrates attacks on marriages. Rising levels of sexual immorality will eventually destroy the foundational fabric of our society – the traditional family and the Covenant of Marriage.

Adultery is a leading cause of marital discord and divorce. I worked with a couple, Jeff and Mary, several years ago who presented a unique set of circumstances. Jeff possessed what one would describe as a very high sexual drive. Jeff was fortunate to share passion with Mary twice a day and almost every day. This level of passionate involvement was evidently just not enough for Jeff, and he became unfaithful. Mary became suspicious of his activities and decided to place a GPS on his vehicle. She was able to track his travels to the homes of various women. Mary caught him in multiple adulterous rendezvous and confronted him. He attempted to lie his way out, but the evidence was overwhelming. He agreed to come to counseling, but was non-responsive for most of the sessions. She was determined not to divorce Jeff, but obviously wanted him to be passionately committed only to her. Her frustration caused her to become creative in reducing Jeff's sexual drive. She made him a large thermos of coffee everyday which he took to work. She discovered when she put one anti-depressant medication in his coffee, there was a noticeable decrease in his sexual activity level. In fact, he got to the point he stayed home much more. I am not aware of how long she did this. I suspect it was just a temporary remedy. I do not recommend this technique. I did admire the dedication that Mary had demonstrated to keep her marriage intact.

Pornography is an incredibly devastating plague upon marriages and our society in general. Pornography is demeaning and dehumanizing to those involved. Pornography attacks the humanity of the individual and degrades them into sexual objects. When I studied the following information, I was shocked by the staggering number of people regularly involved in pornographic activities.

"Pornography hurts adults, children, couples, families, and society. Among adolescents, pornography hinders the development of healthy sexuality, and among adults, it distorts sexual attitudes and social realities. In families, pornography use leads to marital dissatisfaction, infidelity, separation, and divorce."

> ➤ *Every Second*
>   - *28,258 users are watching pornography on the internet*
>   - *$3075.64 is being spent on pornography on the internet*
>   - *372 people are typing the word "adult" into a search engine*
> ➤ *Every Day*
>   - *37 pornographic videos are created in the United States*
>   - *2.5 billion emails containing porn are sent or received*
>   - *68 million search queries related to porn are generated. That accounts for 25% of the total searches on the internet.*
>   - *116,000 queries related to child porn are received*
> ➤ *How Online Pornography Affects Americans*
>   - *200,000 Americans are classified as "pornographic addicts' [I suspect this is way lower than reality.]*
>   - *40,000,000 American people regularly view pornography*
>   - *35% of all internet downloads are related to pornography*
>   - *One-third of pornography views are women. [Which tells me that two-thirds of those who view pornography are men.]*
> ➤ *Family / Marital Porn Stats*
>   - *According the National Coalition for the Protection of Children and Families, 2010, 47% of families in the United States reported porn as a problem in their home.*
>   - *Porn uses increases the marital infidelity rate by 300%*
>   - *40% of people identified as 'sex addicts' lose their spouses, 58% suffer financially, and about 33% lost their jobs.*

- o *68% of divorce cases involve one party meeting a new paramour over the internet.*

[Credit: "Internet Pornography by the Numbers; A Significant Threat to Society"

[Credit Webroot.com]

Pornography is not new. I have viewed murals on the walls of the affluent in ancient Pompeii that portrays pornographic scenes. I have seen the glassware and pottery of the ancient Greeks and Romans that display a perverse expression of 'eros'. King Solomon in Ecclesiastes 1:9 expressed that 'there is nothing new under the sun' and this applies to pornography. The medium has changed but the issue remains the same. 'Eros' was the Greek god of love and sexual desire. Some writers say that he was the offspring of Aphrodite and others says that he and Aphrodite were lovers. Eros translates into Roman culture as Cupid.

The Greek and Roman cultures were replete with inappropriate usage and expression of 'eros'.

The Greek for sexual passion and sensuality is 'eros'. The word 'eros' is absent from the New Testament. The Holy Spirit did not inspire any of the authors of the New Testament to use the word 'eros'. The initial expression of 'eros' in the Original Testament is referred to by various terms such as becoming 'one flesh' [Genesis 2:24,25 -ESV] or 'to know' [Genesis 4:1 – ESV]. In the New Testament the Apostle Paul used the term 'burn' with desire in referencing passion. [I Corinthians 7:9 – ESV] The original intent of our Creator is that 'eros' would be shared by a husband and wife in the safety, sanctity and security of the Covenant of Marriage. By the time the New Testament was written, the purity of 'eros' had become more associated with debauchery.

God invented passion. He created passion for a couple of obvious reasons. One reason to share passion is for procreation. God set into motion His 'after their kind' principle in the Genesis account of creation. God also intended that 'eros' be mutually pleasurable for the husband and wife. Being one flesh and sharing passion and eros appropriately is the most enjoyable physical pleasure for humans. Procreation is necessary for the perpetuation of humanity. God intended for marriages to endure so that parents could train their children and replicate their faith in God to be handed down to future generations.

> *"Did He not make them one,*
> *with a portion of the Spirit*
> *in their union? And what was*
> *the one God seeking?*
> *Godly offspring.*
> *So guard yourselves in your*
> *spirit, and let none of you be*
> *faithless to the wife of your*
> *youth."*
> *[Malachi 2:15 – ESV]*

Hall of Fame NBA basketball legend, Wilt Chamberlain, claimed to have sex with 20,000 women in his life. He revealed this statistic in his 1991 book, A View From Above.

It seems somewhat difficult for the math to add up with reality. If he started his sexual promiscuity at age 18, he would have had to have been with 1.5 women per day for 37 years.

Reports indicate that he enjoyed sexual activity with multiple partners at the same time. He gave an interview in 1999 and offered this final observation just prior to his death on October 12, 1999. And he never backed down on his 20,000 claim.

*"Having a thousand different
ladies is pretty cool, I've learned
in my life. I've found out that
having one woman a thousand
different times is more satisfying."
[Did Wilt Chamberlain Really Sleep
With 20,000 Women" by Eddie
Deezen / Feb. 6, 2018 / Printed
On MentalFloss.com*

Wilt Chamberlain truly lead the life of a popular bachelor according to worldly standards. However, he never married, and the quote above makes me wonder if he came to realize the error of his ways. He would be touted in some circles as 'living the dream'. He was a busy guy, but was he truly happy and satisfied? I am doubtful. Even in personally assessing his sexual exploits, he realized it was more satisfying to be with one woman. In an unusual way, this confirms the design of GOD. I also wonder how many women's lives were negatively impacted by his promiscuity.

Phyllis George interviewed Dallas Cowboy quarterback, Roger Staubach, in 1975.

Comparisons between Staubach and Joe Namath were often debated. Joe Namath stated in a Sports Illustrated article, that I read a long time ago, that he had sexual relationships with 300 coeds at the University of Alabama. Phyllis asked Staubach if he enjoyed sex. I remember watching this interview and Phyllis seemed somewhat taken back by his response. Staubach proclaimed, "I enjoy sex as much as Joe Namath, only I do it with one girl." That 'girl' was his wife, Marianne. [Old Time Football Video].

Passion that is enjoyed as the celebration of the Covenant of Marriage is best described in the Biblical terminology of the 'two becoming one flesh'. Passion is completely knowing your spouse like you know no one else.

Healthy passion involves total physical and emotional bonding. Passion is the ultimate consummation of the pair bonding process. Becoming one flesh and enjoying the eros pleasures of passion is a gift from GOD in the Covenant of Marriage. The goddess of love in Greek mythology was Aphrodite and her male consort was Eros. We derive the English word erotic from Eros. There is nothing wrong with the word erotic when it is shared and enjoyed in the context of the Covenant of Marriage. The misuse of eros and sensuality is epidemic in our culture. Turn on the television tonight and you will view sensual commercials selling cars, clothing, hamburgers and jewelry, etc. The adage that 'sex sells' is promoted in abundance within the advertising community. I remember years ago when 'Dandy' Don Meredith and Howard Cossell were the commentators for Monday night football. This particular Monday the Los Angeles Rams debuted their cheerleaders and their new outfits. The outfits accentuated the breasts very clearly. When 'Dandy' Don saw the cheerleaders he exclaimed something like this: "Now we're giving the people what they want, sex and violence on the same show!!"

Inappropriate use of sensuality is becoming more and more problematic with our youth. Young children are becoming aware of sensuality and sexual activity at a very young age. This type of involvement is stealing their childhood and their innocence. It is causing a perverted view of passion that will impact their dating years and eventually their marriages.

Parents need to monitor what their children are viewing on the internet. There are enormous numbers of sexual and pornographic sites that are easily accessible. I am shocked in counseling how naïve many parents are concerning the necessity to monitor their children. As children mature, they need to be able to discuss sensuality and passion in an age-appropriate context. We can't rely on schools to properly educate our children on the topic of passion.

Passion and its moral expression need to be learned at home and addressed by the church.

Missing Components in the Covenant of Marriage

A good diagnostic and therapeutic tool in counseling is to have the couple assess each of the three components of the Covenant of Marriage: Leave / Cleave / One Flesh. I have them make a personal assessment of how they would personally rate their level of satisfaction on a scale of "1-10"...1 = Poor...and 10 = Perfect.

I also have the couples complete this short exercise to ensure they are understanding accurately the three components. GOD designed the Covenant of Marriage to have three components: Commitment – Intimacy – Passion. Each of these components is important to the vitality of the marriage. Please read each statement and determine which of the three components are present and which are missing.

➢ *A young lady meets her date at her front door for the first time. His statement is:*

"If you don't want to go to bed with me, I don't want to know you!"

[This guy is thinking with the wrong organ!! He is obviously only interested in a Passionate fling. He has zero interest in Intimacy or Commitment.]

➢ *A wife who had been married for six years summarized her relationship with her husband with three words: Married, Sex, and Silence.*

[She and her husband have Commitment and Passion but are severely lacking in the Intimacy component.]

➢ *A TV executive claims, "I am into 'Lite Relationships': All the privileges, half the hassles, and none of the commitments.*

[This executive is only comfortable with a minimal level of Intimacy and a full level of Passion. He has absolutely no interest in Commitment.]

➢ *A young man of twenty-seven reassured his best friend with these words. "Of course it is alright with me if you ask Kim out. We are just good friends."*

[This young man is connected to his best friend in the Intimacy component. But he is not interested in entering into the Covenant of Marriage. He is lacking in Commitment and a desire for Passion. She apparently had higher expectations of their relationship progressing toward the Covenant of Marriage.]

➢ *Dear Abby tells of a woman who was sixty-three years old. This woman had not had sex with her husband for fifteen years. When asked if he would like to go to bed, he replied, "I would rather crush beer cans."*

[They have a Commitment…and only a Commitment. Zero Passion and Intimacy is obviously non-existent for him to respond in that manner.]

➢ *Jack and Ann came to their pastor for counseling to help their marriage. During the sessions, it was discovered that Jack was a caring and faithful husband. But, he had been taught that sex was only for procreation and therefore abstained.*

[This couple has Commitment and Intimacy, but Passion is lacking.]

King Solomon wrote 3,000 proverbs and 917 of those proverbs are contained in the Book of Proverbs. He also wrote 1,000 songs and his best song is recorded in the Song of Solomon. God did not prescribe or endorse polygamy. God did continue to sovereignly work through the lives of those, like King Solomon, who had multiple wives. King Solomon ignored the counsel of God as written in Deuteronomy 17:17 [KJV], "neither shall he multiply wives to himself". The scripture indicates that King Solomon had 700 wives and 300 wives in training known as concubines. But when he wrote his very best song, he dedicated it to one bride. He expresses his love for his Shulamite bride in vivid terms and she reciprocates. Out of the 1,000 women that King Solomon was involved with there was one bride who truly captured his heart.

This accentuates the original intent of God – that one husband would be totally committed to one wife and vice versa and they would seal that commitment with the sharing of 'eros'.

The Song of Solomon is a passionately descriptive book. Some Rabbis in the past would not allow their students to even read this book until they were thirty years old. In this book you will discover the word 'love' used prolifically. The Septuagint is a translation of the Hebrew scriptures into the Greek language that was completed in the second century B.C. The translators of the Septuagint used the word 'eros in many of those instances. This application was meant to describe the sharing of passion between a husband and wife. God puts His stamp of approval on the passionate part of the Covenant of Marriage. Passion is to be enjoyed within the context of the Covenant of Marriage.

The passionate component of the Covenant of Marriage seals the deal as the 'two become one flesh". Sharing passion is the celebration of the Covenant of Marriage and is truly a fantastic gift designed by our Creator.

Conclusion

In this book I have explored three major components that constitute the Covenant of Marriage according to Genesis 2:24,25.

Leave – Commitment – Agape
Cleave – Intimacy – Phileo
One Flesh – Passion – Eros

Early on in this book I mentioned the concept of 'completeness'. The creation of YHWH is replete with examples of symmetry. When YHWH created Adam, he was alone. The other portions of the animal kingdom had male and female counterparts. Adam is a name that refers to humans in general. Adam was asymmetrical in that there was no counterpart for him, humanly speaking. In order to complete Adam YHWH would do a work of rebuilding a perfect counterpart for Adam, a woman. Adam was 'one' and YHWH would take the 'one' and make him 'two'. Adam was unique in his humanity. Eve would be rebuilt from Adam with her own uniqueness and DNA. After Adam was created, he was alone for some time. I am not sure how long Adam was alone, but his feelings were expressed in the opening words of his poem: "This is AT LAST bone of my bones and flesh of my flesh…" [Genesis 2:23 – ESV]

Adam was joyfully relieved that his 'aloneness' had been eradicated.

A Messianic Jewish friend of mine helped me understand the Hebrew words that describe 'man' and 'woman'. This terminology was used in the context of the Covenant of Marriage after Eve was formed. The man, Adam, was then referred to by the Hebrew word 'ish'. "Ish" would have the XY male sex chromosome pattern. "Isha" would be given the XX female chromosome pattern. When these 'two' become 'one' in the context of being 'one flesh' [passion], they complete one another in the fullest sense of this terminology. "Ish" and "Isha" complete one another in the grand design of YHWH. They are no longer alone. Together they can then perpetuate humanity 'after their kind'.

For a marriage to endure, we must resolve to be steadfast and unwavering in our commitment to one another as husband and wife ["Leave"]. We need to continually discover ways to improve the dynamic of intimacy ["Cleave"] with our spouse so that the relationship remains vibrant. Then we mutually celebrate passionately in the safety, sanctity and security of the Covenant of Marriage ["One Flesh"].

My prayer is that husbands and wives will draw close to YHWH and actively seek to complete one another as originally intended by our Creator. May YHWH grant you the ability to meet the needs of your spouse and bring Shalom to your life!!! La Chaim! ><>

In the center of the triangle please be cognizant of the word YHWH. YHWH is the covenant name of God which He revealed to Moses in Exodus 3. YHWH is our Creator and Designer of the Covenant of Marriage. The husband needs to have a personal relationship with YHWH. The wife needs to have a personal relationship with YHWH. Then they both can worship YHWH together and strengthen their marriage so that the Covenant will endure. This personal relationship with YHWH can only be realized by placing your faith in the completed work of Jesus Christ, Yeshua. A marriage that keeps YHWH in the center is a marriage that will last and keep the 'knot' tied. A marriage that is properly functioning is a marriage that brings honor to YHWH. We need to thank YHWH for our spouse and love our spouse in the same way YHWH loves us – sacrificially.

THE WEDDING CEREMONY OF BETHANY JANE CASPER AND KENAN NATHANIEL BELL

May 5, 2012
Officiated by Larry A. Bell, Father of the Groom.
><> A Divine Conspiracy ><>

Deanna and I would like to thank Jody and Sylvia for being Godly parents and raising a woman of faith. We could not have made a better choice for our favorite son. At sundown on 09/28/2011, priests ascended Mount Moriah in Jerusalem and blew the shofar at the Temple Mount announcing the beginning of the Festival of Rosh Hashanah. [Shofar Blast]That shofar blast ushered in the Jewish New Year of 5772. According to the Jewish calendar, this marks the number of years from creation to the present. YHWH made a sovereign decision to speak into existence His creation at that time. There were six days of creation. The first three days He dealt with formlessness as He spoke into existence the life support systems of the air, the sea and the land. The second three days of His creative work He filled those life support systems. The culmination of His creation was man and He then declared HIS creation was very good. God formed man out of the dust of the ground as the Potter molded the clay. A body was formed, but the body was without life until his Creator breathed the breath of life into him and called him Adam.

The breathing of the breath of life is symbolized in the Hebrew culture by the blowing of the shofar, which is GOD summoning to life. Adam, at this point in human history, literally was 'the' man! He was history's first bachelor. Adam took up residence in history's first bachelor pad, a beautiful, garden paradise known as Eden. Adam enjoyed life in a perfect environment. Adam and YHWH had a perfect relationship. Nothing impeded the image-bearer, Adam, from communicating with his Creator – YHWH. I am convinced that YHWH granted Adam a special gift – to communicate with Him just like Moses did eventually – as a friend speaks with a friend. YHWH had expectations and boundaries for Adam. Adam was to tend the garden. He was to prune, cultivate, care and work the ground. He was also to cultivate and mature in his relationship with his Creator. He was also given a special spiritual responsibility. He was to guard the garden. He was to protect his home from the enemy, the adversary. Adam was given a clear expectation and boundary. He was given permission to eat from any of the trees, but there was one special tree – the Tree of Knowledge of Good and Evil – and he was not to eat the fruit of that tree. So, Adam was given Clear Expectations and a Clear Choice. Would he accept what his heavenly Father had in mind for his best interest?

Or would Adam choose to go his own rebellious way? Adam was given Clear Expectations, a Clear Choice, and there would be Clear Consequences. That formula, by the way, is an excellent model for parenting.

Adam was not some sort of Cro-Magnon or Neanderthal caveman running or crawling on all fours. Adam was intelligent and articulate. God assigned him the task of naming the animals that GOD had created. Adam became history's first taxonomist. As Adam studied the animals he made a critical observation. There were male and female lions, male and female camels, and there were male and female ibex. But there was none like that for Adam. You see Adam was alone as a human. Adam had no companion who was like him. Adam had no other person with whom to share his life. This lead YHWH, the Great Physician, to provide history's first diagnosis: "It is not good for man to be alone." It is the first time in recorded human history that the words 'not' and 'good' are used together, assessing the condition of Adam.

The prescribed treatment by YHWH, for the diagnosis of being alone, was history's first usage of anesthesia, as GOD caused a deep sleep to fall upon Adam. The Great Physician then performed history's first operation. HE surgically removed a rib from the side of Adam and fashioned the perfect cure for Adam's condition – history's first woman. She would be the exact treatment that Adam needed. Adam awakened from his GOD-induced sleep and saw his bride. She cared for Adam in the Edenic recovery room and functioned as history's first nurse.

She was named Eve. It's at this point in human history when God, the Father, gave away history's first bride. Adam was so excited and pleased that he was no longer alone that he wrote history's first poem. I can't find any way to determine scripturally how long Adam was alone. But it must have been a significant amount of time as you read and understand the wording of the poem:

"This 'at last' is bone of my bone
and flesh of my flesh.
She shall be called 'woman'
because she was taken out of
man."

This is much more easily understood as a poem in the Hebrew language. And it's the first time in human history where man used the sensitive side of his brain. And some of you ladies in the audience right now are thinking, "and that was the last time!" Guys, take some time and write your lady a letter, write her a poem, or a song, or if you're talented enough maybe you could sing your bride a song. Dust off the sensitive side of your brain and express your emotions and you'll be surprised at the results.

Adam had discovered that he was incomplete in and of himself. Eve was incomplete by herself. They were to come together and complete one another in a divinely inspired partnership known as history's first marriage. It's at this point that Adam was cured. He could now enjoy life more completely and fully. God then records these words in Genesis 2:24,25:

> *"Therefore, shall a man*
> *leave his father and his*
> *mother and shall cleave*
> *unto his wife and they*
> *shall be one flesh. And*
> *they were both naked, the*
> *man and his wife, and they*
> *were not ashamed."*

This section of scripture is also quoted by Christ Himself with a forceful conclusion and warning in Matthew 19:5: "Therefore, what GOD has joined together, let man not separate."

In the Original Testament many contracts and commitments, including marriage, were sealed in a covenant arrangement. The word covenant actually means 'to cut'. Animals were cut and blood sacrifices were utilized. Now we're not going to be cutting any animals today. However, it is with the same type of intensity and sincerity that Kenan and Bethany will enter the Biblical Covenant of Marriage, thereby continuing a scriptural tradition that began 6,000 years ago.

Kenan, a descendant of Adam, 'at last' has found a perfect cure for his loneliness – a beautiful descendant of Eve!

In Genesis 2:24,25 Moses outlines three critical components of a marriage:

Leave – Cleave – and become 'One Flesh'. The word 'Leave' in the Hebrew speaks to the concept of 'Commitment'. Kenan and Bethany as you enter the Covenant of Marriage, you are going to be placing each other in a unique category. Kenan – there should be no woman on planet earth as important to you as this woman. Bethany – there should be no man on planet earth as important to you as this man. You are leaving and changing your social circumstances and forming the basic components of a new family unit. This will require an unwavering and absolutely total commitment to one another. You will need to express unconditional love to one another – agape-type love as described in the New Testament. This is an unconditional love that requires you to honor the vows you will exchange today because you will make these vows in the sight of God and these witnesses. In God's sight it's the right thing to do. Feelings fluctuate but a determination to honor the vows you will take today must not waiver. Unconditional love says I am going to love my spouse in such a way that I am going to give my spouse every type of support, encouragement and challenge to be the best spouse that they can be .and I will do my best to model that type of behavior myself. I will determine to love my spouse in spite of the fact that my spouse is not perfect, recognizing that I am not perfect either. It's a love that will require you to prayerfully seek wisdom and guidance from God.

[Model of Marriage – hand illustration taught to Kenan & Bethany & Witnesses}

Moses then records that after you 'leave' you will 'cleave'. Cleave speaks to intimacy.

Intimacy refers to the emotional bonding that takes place as you continue to develop your relationship. You two began that special emotional bonding on September 25, 2009...953 days ago, on your first date at Ruby Tuesdays in Lynchburg. You must continue to date and put each other on your calendar. Invest quality and quantity time together. You must be willing to talk about everything as you cleave to one another. You need to be best friends. There should be nothing that you two cannot talk about. Physical affection is an important component of the emotional bonding process, and this type of physical affection does not always lead to passion. You have held hands, embraced, kissed, and become very comfortable with each other's physical presence. Appropriate sharing of physical affects proves that you are safe with each other, significant to each other, and secure in your relationship. Your level of emotional bonding and maturing of your relationship needs to strengthen and grow. You must guard against your emotional bonding becoming stagnant. Be considerate and romantically spontaneous with each other. Prove that you care and do not keep score, regarding displaying your kindness to one another. Being reciprocal in sharing acts of kindness will be of terrific benefit in bonding your relationship securely. Keep the romantic flame of intimacy burning brightly.

Moses then records after you 'leave' and 'cleave', then you become 'one flesh'. "One flesh" speaks of passion. The passionate, or sexual part, of the relationship is the most pleasurable experience designed by our Creator. Passion is given as a gift to be expressed in the safety, sanctity, and security of the Covenant of Marriage. It is imperative that you protect the sanctity of your marriage bed. Passion should be a pleasurable experience for both of you and shared frequently enough that you are satisfied with each other... and only each other. In Hebrews 13:4 GOD records these words: "Let the marriage be held in honor among all and let the marriage bed be undefiled..." You need to burn with desire for each other and do not allow the fire of passion to be extinguished.

Paul wrote to the church in Ephesus in Ephesians 5. This is a very special section of scripture to me because on June 7, 2011, this was part of the devotion that my son used at a very special location in Israel. We were in Cana of Galilee at a church that commemorates Christ honoring a wedding and conducting HIS first miracle. This is where Kenan proposed to Bethany...and thankfully she said, "YES"!!!

"Therefore, a man shall leave his father and mother and hold fast to his wife, and the two shall become one flesh. This mystery is profound, and I am saying that it refers to Christ and the church." [Ephesians 5:31,32] Christ is the ultimate picture of the Bridegroom and the church HIS Bride. So, marriage is a type of parabolic teaching – an earthly reality with a spiritual and heavenly application. The Covenant of Marriage continued to be developed after the first marriage in the Garden of Eden. Over the years, the Hebrew culture developed a formalized procedure for the Covenant of Marriage. The initial phase of the marriage covenant was the time of betrothal. The father of the groom to be would talk with his son about the time for him to be ready to select a bride. The son would have input into this decision. Once the potential bride was selected, the father of the groom to be would go to see the father of the potential bride to be and they would make arrangements. The young lady would have input into this decision as well. Details were agreed upon and then money would be exchanged by the father of the groom-to-be to the father of the bride-to-be to offset the loss of services to his home.

Then the father of the groom would take a cup and he would fill it with wine. He would give the cup of wine to his son, who would then offer it to his potential bride. If she drank from the cup, she was willingly entering into the Covenant of Marriage. It's at that point that the marriage became valid and binding. Interestingly, the couple would not take up residence together at that time. The groom would then go to prepare a place for his wife. He would go to the home of his father and he would construct an insula – a special addition to the family home. The groom was responsible for the construction of the insula. The groom was to work diligently. The father of the groom would inspect the work regularly in order to assess the progress. Because it was the father of the groom who would decide when it was time for his son to bring his bride home and take up residence together. During this time, the bride was to spend her time learning her responsibilities and honing her skills for her husband and the children whom she hopes to have at some point as God blesses. She is to be ready and prepared because she does not know when her groom will come to take her home. She is to wait with expectation and excitement. The father of the bridegroom finally inspects the work and declares that the construction is complete. It is at that point that he informs his son that he can go and bring his bride home to live with him forever. The bridegroom then will travel to the village of the bride, accompanied by friends and filled with great joy. He will sound the shofar announcing his arrival and he will take his bride home. The couple will share the wedding feast with family and friends – a terrific time of rejoicing. As you can see here, there is a magnificent spiritual parallel. God, the Father, in eternity past knew that Adam would sin and separate himself from his Creator. And that sin has affected every one of us here today, as sin entered the human experience. Paul writes: "For we have all sinned and fallen short of the glory of God." We are sinners by birth, and we are all sinners by choice.

Thankfully, God did not leave us lost. God made a plan that would bring redemption. Blood atonement was necessary to 'cover' Adam's sin and YHWH covered Adam with garments of skin. But the plan to 'take away' sin would require God sending the 'Second Adam' – Christ Himself. God sent His Son to planet earth to offer Himself as a sacrifice to remove sin. The Bridegroom, YESHUA, accepted the cup of redemption prescribed by His Father and by His crucifixion, He paid the total price to redeem His Bride – the church.

His death, burial and resurrection proved that the price was 'paid in full' for the sin of Adam and all of his descendants. Christ died in victory declaring, "Tetelstai" – "It is finished."

Sin and its consequences could now be 'taken away'. His sacrifice was sufficient for all, but only effective if one believes and applies His blood in faith.

After the resurrection, Jesus the Bridegroom ascended to heaven. He left to go to prepare a place for His bride – the church. HE is now utilizing the skills He learned in His father's carpentry shop in the small village of Nazareth. HE is preparing an insula for His bride situated around the very courtyard of the throne of GOD. One day, a day only known by His Father, He will be told the time has come to bring HIS Bride – the church – home to be with Him forever. The shofar will sound and He will gather His bride to fellowship around the table of the Marriage Feast of the Lamb. John, the Revelator, in Revelation 19:6-9, says these words:

> *"Then I heard what sounded*
> *like a great multitude, like the*
> *roar of rushing waters and like*
> *loud peals of thunder, shouting:*
> *"Hallelujah! For our LORD God*
> *Almighty reigns. Let us rejoice and*
> *be glad and give Him glory! For*
> *the wedding of the LAMB has come,*
> *and His bride has made herself*
> *ready. Fine linen, bright and clean,*
> *was given to her to wear. Fine linen*
> *stands for the righteous acts of God's*
> *holy people.*
> *Then the angel said to me, "Write this:*
> *Blessed are those who are invited to*
> *The wedding supper of the LAMB!"*
> *[NIV]*

Not too many months ago, everyone here received an invitation. That invitation was to come and celebrate the entry into the Covenant of Marriage with Kenan and Bethany. You sent back an RSVP and you are in attendance today. If you want to be part of that 'great multitude', described by John, that assembles around the marriage supper of the

LAMB – you must RSVP to that invitation too. The first recorded question by God to Adam after he fell from grace was this: "Adam, where are you?" That is a question that each of us must answer, "Where are we with God?" Kenan and Bethany want to be sure that you will be there to celebrate that feast as well, just as you are going to celebrate their wedding feast today. You must RSVP by asking Christ to forgive you of your sins... to come into your life and make you a new person. If you do that, you will have a seat at the table because, "Those who call upon the name of the Lord shall be saved." Do you hear the shofar? A summoning by GOD to awaken you to new life. If you hear it - recognize that today is the day of salvation. Will you listen to the shofar of God and allow Him to breathe new life into you and be born again?

When the Jews celebrate Rosh Hashanah, the Jewish New Year, it is a time of retrospection about the previous year. It is a time to assess their life and a call to repentance of those things that are disappointing to God. You may be here today and you already know Christ as your Savior and you can rejoice in the salvation that I have talked about. But you may need to listen to another sounding of the shofar, calling you to a higher level of service, or a call to repent of something that might be disappointing to your Savior. Let Him breathe new life into your relationship with your heavenly Father. And until He sounds that final shofar – summoning us home, which may be soon, may you and I be found faithful, learning, serving, and waiting with great anticipation.

The time has arrived for my favorite son, Kenan, to take his bride, Bethany, home.

The work that you two have done to build your relationship is evidence of your love and devotion to one another. Kenan and Bethany, are you prepared to exchange your vows and enter into the Covenant of Marriage? [Both shake their heads and answer 'yes'].

SHOFAR is Blown

❉❉❉❉❉❉❉❉❉❉❉❉❉❉❉❉❉❉❉❉❉❉❉❉❉❉❉❉❉❉❉❉❉

Kenan & Bethany light the wedding candles
Song:
❉❉❉❉❉❉❉❉❉❉❉❉❉❉❉❉❉❉❉❉❉❉❉❉❉❉❉❉❉❉❉❉❉

Kenan and Bethany, are you prepared to exchange your vows? [Both acknowledged in the affirmative]

In Deuteronomy 23:21–23 Moses records these words:

> *"If you make a vow to the*
> *Lord your God, you shall*
> *not delay fulfilling it for it would*
> *be sin in you and the LORD*
> *your God shall require it of you*
> *and you will be guilty of sin.*
> *But if you refrain from vowing,*
> *you will not be guilty of sin.*
> *You shall be careful to do what*
> *has passed your lips, for you*
> *have voluntarily vowed to the*
> *LORD your God what you*
> *have promised with your mouth."*

To Kenan

Do you proclaim Jesus Christ as your Savior and LORD? [Yes!]

Christ loved the church so much that He sacrificed His life for her, His Bride.

Will you promise to demonstrate such a selfless love for Bethany that you would be willing to lay down your life for her? [I will!]

Do you promise to be the spiritual head of your family – leading by example as you continue to draw ever closer to GOD? [I will!]

To Bethany

Do you proclaim Jesus Christ as your Savior and LORD? [Yes!]

Having heard that Kenan is willing to lay down his very life for you – will you submit to him, as to the LORD? [I will!]

Will you strive to grow ever closer to the LORD in your personal walk with Him?

[I will!]

To Kenan and Bethany

Will you determine to be a peacemaker in your relationship?

[We will!]

Will you make every effort to be patient and kind to one another?

[We will!]

Will you promise to be truthful with each other – recognizing this is a command from God? [We will!]

Will you strive to protect and roof over your marriage as indicated in 1 Corinthians 13?

[We will!]

Will you vow to be best friends and be willing to discuss anything?

[We will!]

Will you covenant to be worthy of each other's trust and be passionately devoted to one another and only one another? [We will!]

Will you promise to keep no record of wrongs – striving to not allow the sun to go down before conflict is resolved? [We will!]

In John 16:33 we read: "In this life you will have trials and tribulation, but take heart, I [CHRIST] have overcome the world." It's not a matter 'if' trials and tribulation will come…but will you vow to be supporting and encouraging to one another in times of trials and tribulation? [We will!]

Will you ask God regularly to empower you to demonstrate an unconditional love to one another? [We will!]

Do you have tokens of your love to exchange today?

[We do!]

And what would those tokens be? [In unison – Rings!]

When you think about a ring, a ring is a very simple design. It has no discernable beginning and no discernable ending. It symbolizes a never-ending existence and it actually speaks to the very presence of God. But in the context of this marriage covenant – it speaks to permanence.

In 1 Corinthians 13:8 Paul writes these words: "Love always perseveres"

The Greek wording there expresses concept of going on a trip. It symbolizes beginning a trip with every intention of completing your journey. Your journey of marriage will begin today by exchanging rings. Your journey of marriage, by the design of God, will not end until you are separated by death. There will be bumps and potholes on this journey which you must avoid and you must not exit. You must determine to 'stay the course'.

Kenan, would you repeat after me? [Nods head – yes!] – "Bethany, you are my beloved, and with this ring I thee wed"/ Kenan – "You are my beloved, and with this ring I thee wed." [Kenan places ring on Bethany's finger]

Bethany, would you repeat after me? [Nods head – yes!] – "Kenan, you are my beloved, and with this ring I thee wed." Bethany – "Kenan, you are my beloved, and with this ring I thee wed." [Bethany places ring on Kenan's finger]

By the authority granted to me by God, through the State of Virginia, I now declare you to be husband and wife...and what God has joined together, let no one tear apart.

Kenan – you may kiss your bride!!! {Cheering and Clapping!!!!}

Let's pray: "Father we come to you in the magnificent name of YESHUA.

We ask Your favor and blessing to come upon Kenan and Bethany and the Covenant they have sealed in Your Name. May they draw close to you and ever closer to each other. May their love and relationship be a testimony to you. In Jesus Name – amen!

[Laid hands on Kenan and Bethany and quoted Numbers 6:24-26]. "The LORD bless thee and keep thee. The LORD make His face shine upon thee and be gracious unto thee. The LORD lift up His countenance upon you and give you peace."

Would you all rise?

"Now to Him Who is able to keep you from stumbling and to present you blameless before the presence of His glory with great joy, to the only GOD, our Savior through Jesus Christ our LORD, be glory, majesty, dominion, and authority, before all time and now and forever. Amen!" And all God's people said:

"Amen"!

Family and friends, it is with an immeasurable amount of joy that I present to you for the first time Mr. and Mrs. Kenan Nathaniel Bell! ><>

Kenan & Bethany Bell exchanging rings – 05/05/2012

Larry Bell officiating wedding of Kenan & Bethany Bell – 05/05/2012

Kenan & Bethany Bell – 05/05/2012

Larry, Kenan, Bethany & Deanna Bell - 05/05/2012

Front Row: Sophia & Violet Gordon
Back Row: Larry, Deanna, Kenan, Bethany & Jessica Bell

Deanna, Kenan, Jessica & Larry Bell - 05/05/2012

Larry & Kenan Bell - May 5, 2012

ADDENDUM

Observations of Some Biblical Marriages
Adam & Eve

The first couple in human history to enter the Covenant of Marriage was Adam and Eve. Adam lived to be 930 years old. Adam and Eve were married a considerable length of time. We can learn from them that the enemy, Satan, desires to bring division and strife into the marriage to destroy the Covenant of Marriage. After Adam deliberately disobeyed GOD, he chose to project blame rather than accept responsibility. When GOD asked Adam in Genesis 3, "Have you eaten of the tree of which I commanded you not to eat?" The man said, "The woman whom you gave to be with me, she gave me the fruit of the tree, and I ate." Adam blamed Eve and actually blamed GOD for giving Eve to him. Essentially Adam was saying: "If You had not given me Eve, I would not be in this situation!" One of the prevalent issues that couples must deal with in marriage counseling is the necessity to accept responsibility for their actions.

We also obtain a clear perspective on the basic tactics Satan uses in spiritual warfare against us. When Satan confronted Eve and tempted her, he appealed to the lust of the flesh, the lust of the eye, and the pride of life.

"For all that is in the world,
the lust of the flesh, and the
lust of the eyes, and the pride
of life, is not of the FATHER,
but is of the world."
[I Joh 2:16 – KJV]

Adam and Eve were the first couple in human history to be attacked by the enemy. We know that the battle being waged against marriages is orchestrated from that same enemy. Satan continues with his desire to destroy marriages and disrupt the traditional family unit. We need to prayerfully fight for our marriages. It is wise to accept the counsel written by the Apostle Peter in I Peter.

"Humble yourselves, therefore,
Under the mighty hand of God
so at the proper time HE may
exalt you, casting all your
anxieties on HIM, because
HE cares for you.
Be sober-minded, be watchful.
Your adversary the devil
prowls around like a roaring
lion, seeking someone to devour.
Resist him, firm in your faith…
[I Peter 5:6,7 – ESV]

The enemy seems to be increasing the intensity of his attacks on the Covenant of Marriage. I suspect that we will continue to experience the expansion of this war until the LORD returns.

When Nehemiah returned from exile in 445 B.C., he was the foreman in charge of the reconstruction of the walls of the city of Jerusalem. He and his fellow countrymen faced opposition from their enemies. Nehemiah was determined to stay the course and he finished the project in fifty-two days. Nehemiah realized what was at stake. A walled city of Jerusalem could be more easily defended. This would allow for residential living and trade to commence.

In the midst of this project Nehemiah offered a challenge to the people of Judah.

> *"I stationed the people by*
> *their clans with swords,*
> *their spears, and their bows.*
> *And I looked and arose and*
> *said to the nobles and to the*
> *officials and to the rest of*
> *the people, "Do not be afraid*
> *of them. Remember the LORD,*
> *Who is great and awesome,*
> *and fight for your brothers,*
> *your sons, your daughters,*
> *your wives, and your homes."*
> *[Nehemiah 4:13,14 – ESV]*

Engage in the battle and fight for your marriage...fight for your family... fight for your home!!!

Moses & Zipporah

Jochebed gave birth to a son, and he was born under a death sentence imposed by the Pharoah of Egypt. All the male Hebrew children were to be executed at birth. The son of Amram and Jochebed was born and secretly hidden for three months. His life was in danger of being extin-guished because of an edict of the government. She took her son to the Nile River and placed him in a basket covered with pitch. As he floated down the Nile, the daughter of Pharoah was bathing and quite likely involved in a worship service to Osiris and Isis – god and goddess of the Nile River. Pharoah's daughter saw the basket in the reeds and instructed her servant to retrieve it. She brought the basket to the daughter of Pharoah. Inside was one of the Hebrew male children. GOD worked in her heart, and she called him Moses and brought him into her home.

Moses spent the first forty years of his life in the home of Pharoah's daughter. He then went to visit his fellow Israelites and saw an Egyptian beating one of his own people. Moses became enraged and killed the Egyptian. Moses fled from Egypt and settled in the land of Midian for the next forty years of his life. When he arrived at Midian, he assisted the seven daugh-ters of Jethro in obtaining water for their flocks. He eventually married Zipporah, one of Jethro's daughters.

Zipporah gave birth to a son whom they named Gershom. Moses was aware of the Abrahamic Covenant and the requirement given by GOD to circumcise his son. However, Moses neglected to circumcise Gershom. It appears from the text in Exodus 4 that Zipporah was likely interfering with the circumcision being performed. The LORD confronted Moses and the circumcision of his son was completed.

A message that comes through this passage is that the husband needs to be the spiritual leader of his family.

Boaz and Ruth

Elimelech and Naomi were married and lived in the small village of Bethlehem approximately 3200 years ago. They had two sons, Mahlon and Chilion. Bethlehem means "House of Bread". A severe famine occurred and, therefore, there was 'no bread in the house'.

The food shortage became so severe that Elimelech moved his family to Moab, which is in modern day Jordan.

As they were trying to make a new life, their sons married Moabite women. Mahlon married Ruth and Chilion married Orpah. Then tragedy struck their family. Elimelech, Mahlon and Chilion all died. Naomi made the decision to return to Bethlehem. She advised her two Moabite daughters-in-law to return to their families and Orpah decided that was in her best interest.

However, Ruth made the opposite decision recorded below.

> *"But Ruth said, "Do not urge me to leave you or to return from following you. For where you go I will go, and where you lodge I will lodge. Your people shall be my people and your GOD my GOD."*
> *[Ruth 1:16 – ESV]*

Ruth made an incredible decision. She decided to place her faith in the same GOD Whom Naomi worshipped – the God of Abraham, Isaac and Jacob. Naomi and Ruth returned to Bethlehem. Naomi then embarked on a match-making mission to obtain a husband for the widowed Ruth.

Naomi was going to work in the context of the Kinsman Redeemer laws of Israel.

Naomi had some land for sale that was owned by Elimelech. The Kinsman Redeemer was required to meet three criteria in order to 'redeem' the land from the widow. First the Kinsman Redeemer had to be related to the deceased. Second, the Kinsman Redeemer had to have enough shekels to financially support the transaction. Third, the Kinsman Redeemer had to be willing.

Ruth had found a job gleaning barley in a field owned by an elderly Hebrew gentleman named Boaz. He was interested in becoming the Kinsman Redeemer for Ruth, but there was a closer relative who had to be contacted to determine his interest and he would have first choice. The relative was contacted and offered his right to purchase the land. Boaz also informed him that if he bought the land, he was responsible to marry Ruth. When he became aware of that stipulation, he was not willing to redeem. Boaz was related, able and willing and he became the Kinsman Redeemer for Ruth and took her as his wife.

YHWH would bless the marriage of Boaz and Ruth and they would become the great-grandparents of King David. YHWH works in mysterious ways through marriages!! Why do you think that an elderly Hebrew named Boaz would want to be the Kinsman Redeemer of a gentile from Moab?? Maybe it was because Boaz had a godly gentile mother named Rahab.

Rehab had placed her faith in the God of Abraham, Isaac, and Jacob and was rescued by Joshua during the battle for Jericho.

When a couple draws close to GOD, and obeys HIM, they invite HIS blessings. GOD does not promise to keep trials and tribulations away from us. GOD does promise to be with us and assist us in navigating through the trials of life.

The ultimate Kinsman Redeemer is YESHUA. YESHUA met all three criteria of the Kinsman Redeemer in order to redeem us from our sins. YESHUA was related to us as the "Word became flesh" and tabernacled among us. YESHUA is omnipotent and, therefore, has all of the resources necessary to redeem. YESHUA was willing to complete the plan of redemption that He and His FATHER had developed from eternity past. Have you been redeemed by YESHUA??

On a side note, YESHUA was born in Bethlehem, the 'House of Bread'. In His teachings at Capernaum, HE referred to Himself as "The Bread of Life". The 'Bread of Life' was born in the 'House of Bread'.

King Ahasuerus and Vashti

King Ahasuerus ruled the large kingdom of Persia that stretched from India to Ethiopia. He was obviously rich and famous. He married a gorgeous Persian lady named Vashti who became his Queen. King Ahasuerus hosted a gala for those in the capital city of Susa. His extravagance was on display for all to see. He had accumulated many valuable possessions of gold, silver, marble, fine linen and even served drinks to his guests in vessels made of gold.

Evidently the guys were in one specific location and Queen Vashti hosted her own party for the ladies. The partying lasted for a prolonged period of time. On day seven of the party the King was intoxicated. His judgment became impaired to some degree.

"On the seventh day, when the

*heart of the king was merry
with wine, he commanded Mehuman,
Biztha, Harbona, Bigtha,
and Abagtha, Zethar, and Carkas,
the seven eunuchs who served in
the presence of King Ahasuerus, to
bring Queen Vashti before the king
with her royal crown, in order to show
the peoples and the princes her beauty,
for she was lovely to look at.
But Queen Vashti refused to come at
the king's command delivered by the
eunuchs. At this time the king became
enraged, and his anger burned
within him."
[Esther 1:10-12 – ESV]*

Queen Vashti made a bold decision to disobey King Ahasuerus and it would cause her to be deposed. She would eventually be replaced by Esther. What were the marital problems between Vashti and Ahasuerus? I believe that there are two major problems that are evident.

King Ahasuerus had just been involved in a prolonged display of his possessions. Now, he was commanding that his 'prize' possession put herself on display before the guys. The King was intoxicated and I'm sure most of the guys had been partying and were inebriated. The King was guilty of treating his wife as something he owned. She was his 'trophy wife' and he must have enjoyed showing her off. Can you imagine the reception she would have received had she agreed to put herself on display? There are some commentators who believe that Vashti was commanded to come display herself only wearing her royal crown. Regardless, the King was treating his wife inappropriately as a possession.

Another issue that is evident in the account is control. The King was attempting to control his wife and 'demanding' that she comply. People do not appreciate being controlled. Wives do not want to feel that their husband is attempting to control them.

*"You don't own me
I'm not one of your many toys
You don't own me
Don't say I can't go with other boys*

*And don't tell me what to do
Don't tell me what to say
And please, when I go out with you
Don't put me on display
["You Don't Own Me –
Lesley Gore -1963]*

Elkanah and Hannah

Elkanah had two wives, Hannah and Peninnah. Peninnah had presented children to Elkanah but Hannah was barren. The tabernacle of YHWH was situated at Shiloh and Elkanah would make a yearly trek to Shiloh to offer a sacrifice to the LORD. The High Priest during this time was Eli. Elkanah loved Hannah and knew she was saddened by the fact she was childless. Elkanah attempted to console Hannah by blessing her with an extra portion of food. He also reassured her of his love for her. Peninnah irritated and provoked Hannah because she had children and Hannah did not.

While worshipping YHWH at Shiloh, Hannah offered a prayer to YHWH and made a vow to HIM. She desperately longed to give birth to a son.

> *"Oh LORD of hosts, if you will*
> *indeed look on the affliction of*
> *your servant and remember me*
> *and not forget your servant,*
> *but will give your servant a son,*
> *then I will give him to the LORD*
> *all the days of his life, and no*
> *razor will touch his head."*
> *[I Samuel 1:11 – ESV]*

YHWH would answer the prayer of Hannah and she would honor her vow. She gave birth to a son named Samuel. Hannah presented her son at the tabernacle of YHWH to enter His service under the guidance of the High Priest. Samuel would be blessed and empowered by YHWH to become the last of the Judges in Israel and the first to hold the office of prophet. Samuel anointed the first two kings of the United Kingdom of Israel, Saul and David. He was a terrific leader and spoke the truth. He confronted King Saul about his incomplete obedience.

When he died, all Israel mourned his passing and he was buried in Ramah. I visited the Tomb of Samuel in June 2019.

The reason I am sharing this account of Elkanah and Hannah is to encourage couples to discuss their intention on having a family. I have had couples who never discussed whether they were planning to have children after they entered the Covenant of Marriage. This can become a major source of contention and strife. I worked with a couple and the wife had just expected that her husband wanted to become a father and he did not. She longed in her heart, like Hannah, to become a mother. GOD was able to intervene and change his heart. This is a critical topic that the couple should discuss while developing the intimacy part of their relationship.

Job & Mrs. Job

In my opinion, the Book of Job is quite likely the oldest book in the Original Testament. Many people think of Job when they think about enduring pain, suffering, and tribulation. Job was attacked by the enemy, Satan himself. Job tragically lost a significant portion of his family. The enemy destroyed a major portion of his material resources. His reputation was being questioned. He then contracted serious health issues. These events caused Mrs. Job to say: "Do you still hold fast your integrity? Curse GOD and die." Mrs. Job offered no words of encouragement and support. She basically advised him to give up.

Job refused to give up and turn his back upon GOD. His reply speaks volumes of his walk with the LORD: "Shall we receive good from GOD, and shall we not receive evil?" In all this Job did not sin with his lips [Job 2:9,10]. We can learn from the determination of Job to be steadfast in our faith. Job was secure in whatever circumstances because he knew GOD.

> *"For I know that my Redeemer*
> *Lives,*
> *and at last he will stand upon the earth.*
> *And after my skin has been thus*
> *destroyed,*
> *yet in my flesh I shall see GOD,*
> *Whom I shall see for myself,*
> *and my eyes shall behold, and*
> *not another."*
> *[Job 19;25-27 – ESV]*

Husbands and wives need to be a source of encouragement to each other.

I would encourage and challenge you to take some time and study more of the Biblical accounts concerning married couples. Abraham lied about his wife Sarah and that could have ended badly without GOD intervening. Samson married a woman who was not good for his spiritual well-being. Esau married out of spite because he was angry at his parents.

The 'Little Old Lady' and the 'Eagle'

The 'Little Old Lady' and the 'Eagle' were quite an effective ministry team. They knew what it was like to suffer under the rule of an anti-Semitic Roman Emperor named Claudius. Claudius abused his considerable authority and evicted all the Jews from the city of Rome. The 'Little Old Lady' and her husband, the 'Eagle', ministered with Paul. They had a church that met in their home. When they were evicted from Rome, they moved to Corinth and set up a tentmaking business. Paul joined them to raise support for his missionary efforts.

The 'Little Old Lady' and the 'Eagle' left Corinth and sailed with Paul to Syria. Paul eventually traveled with them to Ephesus and left them there to minister. They would attend synagogue as followers of YESHUA. In Ephesus they met Apollos who was a fervent believer, but did not have the most current information. They were able to mentor Apollos and help him mature in his walk with YESHUA.

Paul referred to the 'Little Old Lady' and the 'Eagle' as his 'fellow workers'. They served the LORD in such a way to endanger themselves in order to be of assistance to Paul.

Paul further indicated that they had been a considerable blessing to multiple churches throughout Galatia.

The 'Little Old Lady' is commonly referred to as Priscilla. The 'Eagle' is known as Aquila. 'Little Old Lady' and the 'Eagle' are what their names mean in the Greek language.

[See Romans 16; Acts 18; and II Timothy 4:19]

I encourage husbands and wives to find some ways to serve the LORD in ministry together. Early after our conversion in August 1976, my wife and I hosted a house church for twenty-five years. That provided a means of spiritual growth for us and for others. The 'Little Old Lady' and the 'Eagle' provide us with an outstanding example of mutually serving the LORD.

CPSIA information can be obtained
at www.ICGtesting.com
Printed in the USA
LVHW110446170522
718911LV00004B/97

9 781662 841729